Humanism: A Very Short Introduction

VERY SHORT INTRODUCTIONS are for anyone wanting a stimulating and accessible way into a new subject. They are written by experts, and have been translated into more than 45 different languages.

The series began in 1995, and now covers a wide variety of topics in every discipline. The VSI library now contains over 500 volumes—a Very Short Introduction to everything from Psychology and Philosophy of Science to American History and Relativity—and continues to grow in every subject area.

Titles in the series include the following:

Stephen Law

HUMANISM

A Very Short Introduction

OXFORD
UNIVERSITY PRESS

OXFORD

UNIVERSITY PRESS

Great Clarendon Street, Oxford OX2 6DP

Oxford University Press is a department of the University of Oxford.
It furthers the University's objective of excellence in research, scholarship,
and education by publishing worldwide in

Oxford New York

Auckland Cape Town Dar es Salaam Hong Kong Karachi
Kuala Lumpur Madrid Melbourne Mexico City Nairobi
New Delhi Shanghai Taipei Toronto

With offices in

Argentina Austria Brazil Chile Czech Republic France Greece
Guatemala Hungary Italy Japan Poland Portugal Singapore
South Korea Switzerland Thailand Turkey Ukraine Vietnam

Oxford is a registered trade mark of Oxford University Press
in the UK and in certain other countries

Published in the United States
by Oxford University Press Inc., New York

British Library Cataloguing in Publication Data

Data available

Library of Congress Cataloging in Publication Data

Data available

Typeset by SPI Publisher Services, Pondicherry, India
Printed and bound by
CPI Group (UK) Ltd, Croydon, CR0 4YY

ISBN: 978-0-19-955364-8

Contents

Acknowledgements

I would like to thank, in particular, Andrew Copson (Chief Executive of the British Humanist Association) and Ronald Lindsay (Executive Director of the Center for Inquiry) for their detailed comments on earlier drafts of this book. Their help has been invaluable. The book is, however, entirely my own responsibility and should not be assumed to represent the views of any other individual, or any particular humanist organization.

I would also like to thank (alphabetically) David Papineau, David Pollock (President of the European Humanist Federation), John Shook, Reginald Williams, an anonymous reader for OUP, and finally the readers of my blog <http://www.stephenlaw.org>, for helpful comments and suggestions.

List of illustrations

Introduction: what is humanism?

The word 'humanism' has had, and continues to have, a variety of meanings. At its broadest, 'humanism' means little more than a system of thought in which human values, interests, and dignity are considered particularly important. Understood in this way, perhaps almost everyone qualifies as a humanist (including those of us who are religious).

However, those who organize under the banner of 'humanism' today, especially in the UK, usually mean something rather more focused. They embrace a particular kind of worldview that by no means everyone accepts. That worldview is the focus of this book.

So what distinguishes the humanist outlook? It is difficult to be very precise. The boundaries of the concept are elastic. But I think most humanists would probably agree on something like the following minimal, seven-point characterization (in no particular order):

First, humanists believe science, and reason more generally, are invaluable tools we can and should apply to all areas of life. No beliefs should be considered off-limits and protected from rational scrutiny.

Second, humanists are either atheists or at least agnostic. They are sceptical about the claim that there exists a god or gods. They are also sceptical about angels, demons, and other such supernatural beings.

Third, humanists believe that this life is the only life we have. We are not reincarnated. Nor is there any heaven or hell to which we go after we die. Notice that the humanist's sceptical position regarding both gods and an afterlife is not a dogmatic 'faith position', but a consequence of their having subjected such beliefs to critical scrutiny and found them seriously wanting.

Fourth, humanism involves a commitment to the existence and importance of moral value. Humanists also believe our ethics should be strongly informed by study of what human beings are actually like, and of what will help them flourish in this world, rather than the next. Humanists reject such negative claims as that there cannot be moral value without God, and that we will not be, or are unlikely to be, good without God and religion to guide us. Humanists offer moral justifications and arguments rooted other than in religious authority and dogma.

Fifth, humanists emphasize our individual moral autonomy. It is our individual responsibility to make our own moral judgements, rather than attempt to hand that responsibility over to some external authority – such as a political leader or religion – that will make those judgements for us. Humanists favour developing forms of moral education that emphasize this responsibility and that will equip us with the skills we will need to discharge it properly.

Sixth, humanists believe our lives can have meaning without it being bestowed from above by God. They suppose that the lives of, say, Pablo Picasso, Marie Curie, Ernest Shackleton, and Albert Einstein were all rich, significant, and meaningful, whether there is a God or not.

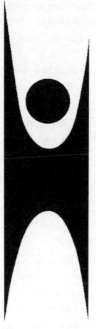

1. The happy human symbol has been adopted by both the British Humanist Association and the International Humanist and Ethical Union, to which many humanist organizations around the world belong

Seventh, humanists are secularists, in the sense that they favour an open, democratic society in which the state takes a *neutral* position with respect to religion, protecting the freedom of individuals to follow and espouse, or reject and criticize, both religious and atheist beliefs. While humanists will obviously oppose any attempt to coerce people into embracing religious belief, they are no less opposed to coercing people into embracing atheism, as happened under certain totalitarian regimes.

3

There are a number of other views sometimes also associated with humanism that I have not included here. Note, for example, that, as characterized here, a humanist need not:

- be a utopian, convinced that the application of science and reason will inevitably usher in a Brave New World of peace and contentment.

- believe that *only* humans matter, morally speaking. Many humanists consider that the happiness and welfare of other species are also important.

- be a utilitarian – supposing that maximizing happiness and minimizing suffering are all that matter, morally speaking. While some humanists embrace utilitarianism, and almost all believe that happiness and suffering are morally important, not all humanists are utilitarians.

- embrace those brands of naturalism that say that the natural, physical universe is the only reality there is, and/or that the natural, physical facts are the only facts that there are. Many humanists, perhaps the majority, embrace some form of naturalism. Some even define their brand of 'humanism' as involving naturalism. However, the looser definition employed here allows humanists to criticize naturalism if they wish. Yes, humanists reject, or are at least agnostic concerning, belief in gods, angels, demons, and so on, but that doesn't require that they sign up to naturalism. Take, for example, a mathematician who believes that mathematics describes a non-natural, mathematical reality (a sort of numerical heaven). This mathematician rejects naturalism, but that does not entail they cannot be a humanist. Or take a philosopher who believes they have established that, say, moral facts, or the facts about what goes on in our conscious minds, are facts that exist in addition to all of the natural, physical facts. Again, I see no reason why such a philosopher cannot be a humanist. A recent survey revealed that while only 14.6% of professional philosophers believe in God, just under 50% of them are committed to naturalism. I consider it unnecessarily restrictive to define 'humanism' in such a way as automatically to exclude the significant proportion who fail to believe in either gods or naturalism.

- embrace scientism, believing that every genuine question can in principle be answered by science. Take moral questions, for example. Humanists can, and often do, accept that, while scientific discoveries can inform our moral decisions, science and reason alone are incapable of determining what is morally right or wrong. A humanist may suppose that other questions – such as 'Why is there anything at all?' – are also *bona fide* questions that science cannot answer. Humanists are merely sceptical about *one particular answer* – that the universe is the creation of one or more gods.

In order to refute humanism as I have characterized it, then, it is not enough that one refute utopianism, utilitarianism, scientism, or naturalism. A humanist can reject, or remain neutral concerning, all these philosophical stances.

Humanists are sometimes criticized for not being 'for' anything. They are often caricatured as naysayers, defined entirely by what they oppose – belief in a god or gods.

However, notice that even the theist rejects belief in the countless *other* gods people have believed in down through the centuries (such as those of the Ancient Romans, Greeks, Norse, Mayans, Egyptians, and so on). The humanist merely remains unconvinced of the existence of one or two more.

Moreover, notice that, as outlined here, humanism goes far beyond mere atheism or agnosticism, and is clearly *for* a great deal.

For example, humanism is for freedom of thought and expression and an open society. Humanism is for forms of moral education

5

that stress our moral autonomy and the importance of thinking critically and independently. Humanists don't just reject dogma-based approaches to answering moral, political, and social questions, they are very much for developing positive, rational, and ultimately more life-affirming and life-enhancing alternatives.

Humanist thinking is also sometimes caricatured as a hodgepodge of disparate, unconnected ideas – but again, this is untrue. Humanism's focus is on the 'big questions', for example of what ultimately is real; of what ultimately makes life worth living; of what is morally right or wrong, and why; and of how best to order our society. While religion typically addresses such questions, they are clearly not the unique preserve of religion. Such questions also belong to philosophy, and were being addressed in a rational, non-religious way before the appearance of Christianity. What pulls our seven characterizing views together into something like a *system* of thought is (i) their shared focus on the 'big questions', (ii) a degree of interconnectedness (for example, if you are sceptical about gods, that will lead you to be sceptical about the claim that our moral sense was placed in us by a god), and (iii) the over-arching role played by the first: these views on the 'big questions' are collectively embraced, not as a dogmatically held 'faith position', but because, having subjected the various alternatives to rational scrutiny, the humanist considers these the most *reasonable* positions to adopt.

Finally, I want to say something about humanist antipathy to religion. Clearly, many humanists consider religion, not just false, but dangerous. Some even view religion as a great evil. But not all. A significant number of religious people actually share many of the views in terms of which I have characterized humanism. They too are secularists. They also accept that morality and a meaningful life are possible even in the absence of a god. They may also share many of the same goals as humanists. Many humanists are happy to work in conjunction with religious people and organizations to achieve such goals. And of course, there are religious people willing to work in conjunction with humanists. At the time of writing, the Bible Society's think tank Theos donated towards a British Humanist Association advertising campaign promoting the idea that children should not be labelled with a religion, but should be allowed to grow up free to make their own decisions about which religion, if any, to embrace. Humanists and religious people obviously disagree on certain fundamental issues. But there is often a great deal on which they can agree. There is no particular reason why humanist organizations cannot develop constructive working partnerships with their religious counterparts.

This book aims to further explain, and begin to make a case for, humanism, as characterized above.

Chapter 1
History of humanism

The roots of modern humanism run at least as far back as the Ancient world. The kind of 'big questions' humanism addresses – such as 'does God exist?', 'what makes for a meaningful life?', and 'what makes things morally right or wrong?' – are questions humanity has been asking the world over for millennia. In many times and places, both the approach taken to answering such questions and the non-religious answers given have been similar to the approach taken and answers given by humanists today. As we are about to discover, modern humanism is able to draw on a rich and long intellectual legacy.

Ancient Indian thought

A sceptical attitude towards religious teaching is a feature of some early Indian writing. One of the Upanishads even questions whether the god Brahman exists. Later, a 6th-century BC Indian school of thought – the Carvaka system – did not merely question whether there was a deity, it positively asserted that there was not. The Carvaka school of philosophy is essentially atheistic and materialistic, insisting the natural, material world is all that there is, priests are useless, and religion a false human invention. Rather than lead an ascetic existence, we should live life to the full, seeking out pleasure and happiness. The Carvaka school illustrates the point that a sceptical attitude towards all religious beliefs is neither a recent, nor a peculiarly Western, phenomenon.

Confucius

Confucius (551–479 BC) is the father of Confucianism, a system of thought that came to dominate China and other parts of Asia for millennia. Although Confucius took the existence of both heaven and gods for granted, the system of ethical and political philosophy he developed stood in large part independently of any commitment to gods and supernaturalism. Confucius is particularly associated with the Golden Rule. He said:

> Do not unto another that you would not have him do unto you.
> Thou needest this law alone. It is the foundation of all the rest.

The Golden Rule is embraced not only by many religious people (it is, of course, also associated with later religious figures, including Jesus), but also by many humanists.

Ancient Greece

Ancient Greece witnessed an extraordinary flowering of human culture, and the systematic application of reason to various fundamental social, moral, and political questions. This questioning, critical attitude led some to reject belief in gods.

Ancient Greece is also significant to contemporary humanists because it exhibits political developments important to humanism – most notably a limited form of *democracy* (though forms of democracy may have existed earlier, for example in 6th-century BC India). Some Greek states – especially Athens – were also comparatively *open*, largely tolerating the questioning of orthodoxy and the promotion of a wide variety of philosophical views.

Three early Greek philosophers – Thales, Anaximander, and Anaximenes – are of particular interest. The manner in which these Milesian philosophers thought critically and independently, largely putting aside mythological and religious explanations and instead attempting to develop their own ideas and theories grounded in observation and reason, obviously makes them particularly important from a humanist point of view. They collectively exhibit several of the key ideas and values of humanism. Many consider Anaximander the father of astronomy. He developed an essentially mechanical model of how the heavens operate, in contrast to the largely mythological explanations previously offered. Anaximander also developed a theory, based partly on fossils, that man developed from creatures that lived in the sea.

Another significant philosopher, from a humanist perspective, is Protagoras (490–420 BC). His reasoning about morality and virtue was pursued without any reliance on theistic or religious doctrine or belief. Protagoras was a self-declared agnostic. He said:

> Concerning the gods, I have no means of knowing whether they exist or not or of what sort they may be, because of the obscurity of the subject, and the brevity of human life.

The doctrine with which Protagoras is now most closely associated is,

> Man is the measure of all things, of the reality of those which are, and the unreality of those which are not.

The Greek philosopher Plato interpreted Protagoras to mean that what is true and what is false is relative to individuals and what they believe. If I believe that Paris is the capital of France, then that is *true for me*; if you believe Berlin is the capital of France, than that is *true for you*. There is *no objective fact of the matter* – no truth with a capital 'T', as it were – as to which of us is correct.

Note that, on such a crude, relativistic view of truth, it is possible to make something true just by believing it. (Want to be able to fly? You need only believe that you can.) Plato famously attacks this form of relativism in his dialogue *Theaetetus*, where he points out that if relativism is true, then it is only relatively true. Plato can make it false just by believing it to be so.

Protagoras' supposedly relativistic views are not merely of historical interest. The same brand of relativism is supposedly widespread today. The American academic Allen Bloom once wrote:

> [t]here is one thing a professor can be absolutely certain of: almost every student entering university believes, or says he believes, that truth is relative.

Indeed, relativism is widely supposed to be something like an sickness infecting contemporary society and undermining its morality. For example, when US troops were found to have tortured Iraqi civilians at Abu Ghraib, Colorado's Governor Richard Lamm said:

> This reflects a breakdown in society. These people's moral compass didn't work for some reason. My guess is because they've been infected with relativism.

The current pontiff has expressed similar concerns:

> We are moving towards a dictatorship of relativism which does not recognize anything as for certain and which has as its highest goal one's own ego and one's own desires.

This contemporary anxiety about relativism has had an impact on educational policy, with, for example, Nick Tate, Chief Executive of the UK's Qualifications and Curriculum Authority, saying (in the context of the introduction of citizenship classes to the national curriculum):

If ever a dragon needed slaying, it is the dragon of relativism.

The extent to which relativism really is widespread is controversial. However, it's worth noting that relativism is not a recent phenomenon, and that it was debated even in Ancient times.

Contemporary humanists are often caricatured by their opponents as subscribing to relativism, particularly *moral* relativism – the view that the truth about what is morally right or wrong is whatever the individual or community believes it to be. However, as I explain in Chapter 4, humanists are opposed to relativism generally, and to moral relativism in particular.

Aristotle (384–322 BC) is also significant to humanists, not least because he attempts to develop a rational, ethical theory rooted in a close study of the nature of human beings, and because the focus of his ethics is on how to achieve a particular kind of happiness or wellbeing in this life (rather than in some life to come). Aristotle's virtue ethics – which focuses on the importance of developing good character, rather than on rules or consequences – is influential among contemporary ethicists, including some humanist ethicists.

But perhaps the most important Ancient Greek philosopher, from the point of view of humanism, is Epicurus (341–271 BC). Epicurus was a materialist who believed, like the philosopher Democritus, that matter was made up of invisible parts or atoms existing in empty space and governed by laws. Human beings too are essentially corporeal, according to Epicurus, possessing no immaterial or immortal soul. According to Epicurus, justice consists in our abiding by the contracts and agreements we make between us not to harm each other.

For Epicurus, philosophy is essentially therapeutic. His aim was the development of a philosophy of life that would allow us to enjoy a happy and tranquil existence free from fear.

2. Epicurus

While Epicurus took the existence of gods for granted, he supposed they could have no interest in human affairs. They neither rewarded nor punished us, so there was no need to fear them. Nor should death be feared, thought Epicurus, because once we are dead, we no longer exist to experience anything. But then there is nothing in death – no pain or suffering – for us to fear. Epicurus' saying:

> I was not; I have been; I am not; I do not mind

was often inscribed on the gravestones of his followers, particularly throughout the Roman Empire. It can often be heard recited at humanist funerals today.

Epicurus placed particular emphasis on friendship and living well. He also believed that pleasure and pain were the only measures of good and bad. As a result, Epicurus has often been misunderstood as recommending a life of unbridled hedonism – of gluttony and orgies. In fact, Epicurus warns against overindulgence and excess. He is significant to humanists because he develops an approach to leading a good life entirely independently of any concerns about gods or the supernatural.

The Roman Empire

The Ancient Roman Empire also produced a number of thinkers who, to varying degrees, expressed a broadly humanist outlook.

Cicero (106–43 BC), for example, was a sceptic, believing that knowledge about the gods was impossible. He believed ethical values are independent of institutionalized religion, and are amenable to rational, philosophical enquiry.

The Roman philosopher Seneca (2 BC–AD 65) believed that:

> Religion is recognized by the common people as true, by the wise as false, and by the rulers as useful.

Like most modern-day humanists, he also insisted that 'the time to live is now'.

Averroës

During the medieval period, Europe was largely dominated by Christian thought. Almost all artistic and intellectual endeavour was theologically orientated. The questioning of religious orthodoxy was rarely tolerated, and was often met with violence and persecution.

Within the Arab world, however, could be found more liberal intellectual trends. The Arab thinker Averroës (1126–98) was born in Cordoba in Islamic Spain, an area remarkable for its comparative intellectual freedom. Averroës' clear and accessible commentaries on Aristotle were an important influence on European Christian thinkers who were rediscovering the works of Aristotle, largely lost to Christian Europe since the 6th century. Indeed, the Christian thinker Thomas Aquinas (1225–74) refers to Aristotle as 'the philosopher' and Averroës as 'the commentator'.

Averroës argued that, where religious scripture is contradicted by what philosophers such as Aristotle had revealed, scripture should be reinterpreted as allegorical. This comparatively radical and liberal approach to religious texts, in effect giving science and reason the authority to challenge scripture as literally understood, was snuffed out within the Arab world. But Averroës had sown an important, liberalizing seed in Western thought – where discussions of how faith and philosophy might be reconciled were to become increasingly important.

The Renaissance

The Renaissance (literally 'rebirth' in French) spans the 14th to the later 16th or early 17th centuries, beginning in Florence in Italy. The movement was partly brought about by a renewed interest in Classical thought. The ideas and arguments of Ancient Greek and Roman thinkers were sought out, and gave enormous impetus to intellectual inquiry, which now broadened out far beyond the boundaries of Christian theology. The visual arts, which had been largely focused on religious subject matter, now broadened in their scope, becoming much more naturalistically orientated, as well as drawing on Classical mythologies in addition to Jewish and Christian ones. Drawing in perspective was developed. Leonardo da Vinci's (1452–1519) studies of human physiognomy, which informed his artistic portrayal of the human form, nicely illustrate the way in which the study of the human and human culture came much more to the fore during the Renaissance.

There were important religious upheavals too. There was growing criticism of the Catholic Church, which was increasingly perceived to be corrupt, especially in its sale of indulgences, which granted heaven-bound purchasers remission of punishment in purgatory. In 1517, Luther (1483–1546) published his *Ninety-Five Theses on the Power and Efficacy of Indulgences*. The development of the printing press allowed such new and radical ideas to be distributed widely. Luther's attempts to reform the Catholic Church eventually resulted in the Reformation and the creation of Protestantism, bringing to an end the Catholic Church's religious dominance of Europe.

During the Renaissance, the modern scientific method was developed, perhaps most notably by Francis Bacon (1561–1626). And of course, the Renaissance also saw some famous scientific challenges to religious thought. Giordano Bruno (1548–1600) was a polymath Dominican who defended the Copernican view that the Earth moved around the Sun. Bruno was interrogated by the Inquisition about both his cosmological and also other unorthodox religious views, and was eventually burned at the stake. One of the most dramatic incidents illustrating growing tensions between scientific and religious thought involved the astronomer and physicist Galileo (1564–1642). Galileo had been warned by the Catholic Church not to assert that Copernicus' heliocentric model was literally correct (it could be used only as a useful predictive tool). Galileo nevertheless did so, and in a rather provocative way. As a result, Galileo was arrested and threatened with torture and execution by the Holy Inquisition. After Galileo recanted, he was merely imprisoned, a sentence later commuted to house arrest.

A number of modern Catholic commentators insist it would be unfair to characterize the Catholic Church as being anti-science at this time. Some maintain it was Bruno's theological views, not his cosmological views, that got him into trouble with the Inquisition. However, that claim is not born out by the Vatican's own archives, which clearly indicate Bruno was interrogated about his cosmological views. Some commentators also maintain Galileo was arrested, not for his scientific views, but merely for his views concerning the interpretation of scripture. But this is disingenuous. Because Galileo maintained the Earth moved around the Sun, he had no choice but to say either that scriptural claims to the contrary were simply mistaken (which would, of course, have been suicidal), or that those parts of scripture that *appeared* to claim the Earth did not move would need to be reinterpreted.

In fact, some Catholic theologians, such as Cardinal Bellarmine, who was charged with investigating Galileo, conceded that, were it conclusively proved that the Earth moved, then scripture *might* have to be reinterpreted. The problem was, Galileo possessed no conclusive proof.

So, to characterize the Catholic Church's position at that time as *wholly* entrenched and insensitive to new scientific developments would be to exaggerate somewhat. Nevertheless, it appears the Church was willing to torture and kill any scientist prepared publicly to contradict its Earth-centred cosmology without possessing conclusive scientific proof.

Of course, the overwhelming majority of religious people now entirely accept that the application of science and reason in trying to understand how our universe works should not be subject to any sort of religious censorship or control. In 2000, Pope John Paul II publicly apologized for, among other things, the Church's trial of Galileo. However, in 1990, Cardinal Ratzinger – now Pope Benedict XVI – quoted philosopher Paul Feyerabend, seemingly with approval:

> At the time of Galileo the Church remained much more faithful to reason than Galileo himself. The process against Galileo was reasonable and just.

Precisely what Ratzinger meant by this remark is a matter of debate, but it obviously raised a few humanist eyebrows.

The Enlightenment

The European Enlightenment – sometimes known as the 'Age of Reason' – spans from the late 17th century to the end of the 18th century. The Enlightenment saw increased criticism of traditional religious beliefs and institutions from new, more radical religious groups. This resulted in the fragmentation of Christianity into further denominations. But while there was criticism of religious belief, this tended to come from the point of view of alternative religious beliefs. Atheistic beliefs were still rarely heard, and in many places to espouse such beliefs was to risk persecution.

In mid-18th-century France, the Enlightenment *philosophes'* Denis Diderot (1713–84) and Jean D'Alembert (1717–83) published the *Encyclopaedia*, an edited compendium of knowledge which contained many radical liberal, naturalist, and sceptical ideas. Diderot was an atheist, and both men were highly critical of organized religion. The book was banned before its completion. As an intellectual movement, the Enlightenment has been characterized in a variety of ways. Diderot and D'Alembert defined the Enlightened thinker as one who

> trampling on prejudice, tradition, universal consent, authority, in a word, all that enslaves most minds, dares to think for himself.

But perhaps the best-known definition of Enlightenment comes from the philosopher Immanuel Kant (1724–1804), who in 1784 wrote a short magazine article titled 'What is Enlightenment?' Kant characterizes Enlightenment as

> [e]mergence of man from his self-imposed infancy. Infancy is the inability to use one's reason without the guidance of another. It is self-imposed, when it depends on a deficiency, not of reason, but of the resolve and courage to use it without external guidance. Thus the watchword of the Enlightenment is *Sapere Aude!* Have the courage to use one's own reason!

Some Enlightenment thinkers stand accused of *utopianism*, of naively supposing that the age of reason would inevitably bring in an age of peace, prosperity, and contentment. Enlightenment thought is also accused of being excessively *rationalistic*, of supposing society and morality can be given a *wholly* rational foundation. This, it is now widely held, was a mistake: the rabbit of morality cannot be conjured entirely out of the hat of reason. Many critics of the Enlightenment would add this was a dangerous mistake: the result of kicking away the old foundations of religious authority and tradition was to leave morality and society without any foundations at all – a recipe for disaster.

However, while some Enlightenment thinkers were indeed utopian, and some, such as Kant, supposed morality could be founded upon reason alone, notice that *neither of these beliefs is entailed by Kant's characterization of Enlightenment.* To believe in the importance of raising Enlightened citizens in Kant's sense of the term – citizens who dare to think and question, who apply their powers of reason as far as they are able rather than just passively, uncritically accept what they are told by some religious or other authority – is not to sign up to utopianism or to suppose morality and society can be given wholly rational foundations. Modern humanism clearly involves a commitment to Enlightenment in Kant's sense. That does not mean that today's humanists are utopians, or that they inevitably overestimate what reason is able to do (though both charges are regularly levelled at contemporary humanism).

Another popular criticism of many Enlightenment thinkers is that they falsely supposed that reason can be applied without appeal to a shared tradition. As we have seen, Diderot and D'Alembert define the Enlightened thinker as one who 'tramples' on tradition. But this, many philosophers have argued, is an incoherent view, as whatever forms of reasoning we employ *will themselves be born of and be dependent upon a shared tradition*. For example, according to the contemporary philosopher Alistair MacIntyre,

> [A]ll reasoning takes place within the context of some traditional mode of thought.

It is not possible, claims MacIntyre, to 'step outside' of all tradition and to reason from an entirely tradition-free perspective. So, on MacIntyre's view, it's actually impossible to do what D'Alembert and Diderot encourage us to do: to apply reason on an individual basis, independently of any tradition.

However, even if MacIntyre is correct, it does not follow that we ought not to question traditional thinking. MacIntyre himself is clear about this, insisting that

> [n]othing can claim exemption from reflective critique.

It is one thing to say that, in applying reason, we cannot help but draw on a tradition. It is quite another to say that we ought not to examine traditional beliefs too critically. Kant's injunction that we should dare to question and think for ourselves, rather than uncritically accept the pronouncements of tradition, remains unthreatened. It is that Enlightenment injunction that today's humanists embrace.

A particularly important Enlightenment thinker, from the point of view of humanism, is David Hume (1711–76). Hume was a brilliant Scottish historian and philosopher who subjected many supposedly common-sense beliefs to critical scrutiny – including religious beliefs. He was sceptical about religious and other miracles. Hume's *Dialogues Concerning Natural Religion*, published after his death, contain some of the most devastating critiques ever devised of the so-called 'arguments from design' for the existence of God. Whether Hume was an agnostic or an atheist remains contentious – but he did not believe in God.

Hume raised some important questions about *the limits of reason*. He argued that moral beliefs were ultimately not justifiable by appeal to either reason or experience, maintaining that

> It is not contrary to reason to prefer the destruction of the whole world to the scratching of my finger.

Hume also argued that inductive reasoning, upon which all our beliefs about the future, and the empirical sciences, are founded, cannot be rationally justified. Given that we have seen the Sun rise every morning, we believe it will rise tomorrow morning. Indeed, we cannot help but believe this. Nevertheless, argues Hume, we are no more *justified* in supposing the Sun will rise tomorrow morning than we would be if, say, we supposed a huge million-mile-wide bowl of tulips will appear over the horizon instead.

Most contemporary humanists agree with Hume that, while we should apply reason wherever we can and as best we can, reason has its limits (though whether or not these limits fall quite where Hume supposed is contentious).

The 19th century

In 1859, Charles Darwin (1809–82) published his *Origin of Species*, which explained how new species evolved over many millions of years. Prior to Darwin, it was widely supposed that species could only be created by God. Indeed, Enlightenment thinkers had not possessed an alternative explanation of how species might be created. Darwin explained how purely natural, scientifically investigable mechanisms were capable of producing new species – a very dramatic development. Indeed, that species had evolved in this way was strongly supported by the evidence, which of course flatly contradicted the biblical account.

The 19th century also saw important developments in biblical criticism, particularly in Germany. German scholars such as David Strauss (1808–74) and Julius Wellhausen (1844–1918) were beginning to reveal the mythical character of much of the Bible. Also in Germany, the theologian and philosopher Ludwig Feuerbach (1804–72) rejected orthodox religious ideas, insisting that the god of conventional religion was merely the illusory, outward projection of mankind's inner nature, and Friedrich Nietzsche (1844–1900) railed against Christian morality, accusing it of being life-stunting and born of feelings of hatred and resentment. And of course, the German Karl Marx (1818–83) suggested religion was 'the opiate of the masses'.

In Britain, the philosophers Jeremy Bentham (1748–1832) and John Stuart Mill (1806–73) developed a radical ethical theory called utilitarianism that defined moral goodness in terms of happiness. According to Bentham, 'the greatest happiness of the greatest number is the foundation of morals and legislation'. One radical feature of utilitarianism is the way in which it dispenses with the need to introduce any sort of supernatural being in order to underpin or account for morality. According to the utilitarian, in order to evaluate the extent to which something is morally right or wrong, we need not focus on anything other than what takes place in *this*, the *natural*, world. For many religious people, such views were, and are, shockingly beyond the pale. Many of the customs, laws, and institutions of Bentham's day caused misery to many. Utilitarianism suggests that not only is it desirable to alleviate suffering where we can, it is actually a moral requirement. Utilitarianism thus led, and continues to lead, many utilitarians towards legal and social reform. Bentham's utilitarianism led him to believe that, because other creatures suffer too, we are also under moral obligations to them. About other animals, Bentham said:

> the day may come when the rest of the animal creation may acquire
> those rights which never could have been witholden from them
> but by the hand of tyranny.

By no means all contemporary humanists are utilitarians. However, the development of utilitarianism was clearly of importance to the development of modern humanism, not least because it provides yet another illustration of how an intellectually robust and sophisticated view of morality can be articulated and defended quite independently of any religious belief.

The censorship and persecution of non-believers still existed in Europe. The year 1826 saw the last victim of the Holy Inquisition executed in Spain (school teacher Cayetano Ripoll was garrotted for supposedly teaching Deist ideas). In 1842, G. J. Holyoake (1817–1906) (who first coined the term 'secularism') was the last (and perhaps also the first) person in Britain to be imprisoned on a charge of atheism. However, increasing numbers of public figures were prepared publicly to doubt the claims of religion. In Britain, the writers Percy Bysshe Shelley (1792–1822), George Eliot (1819–80), and Thomas Hardy (1840–1928) were openly atheist. In 1880, Charles Bradlaugh (1833–91), joint founder of the National Secular Society in 1866, was elected Britain's first openly atheist member of Parliament (though his atheism meant he could not take the Oath of Allegiance, and so he was barred from taking his seat for several years).

3. Conway Hall, Red Lion Square, home of the South Place Ethical Society

The 19th century saw the rise of ethical societies, which sprang up in both Europe and the United States. These societies provided a framework within which people could discuss ethical matters and engage in ethical activity – such as charitable work and social and educational programmes. They were free-thinkers, encouraging open debate about ethical and religious matters. While many ethical societies described themselves as 'religious', they were often religious only in the sense that they took their ethical commitments seriously – belief in a deity was optional. Felix Adler (1851–1933), founder of the New York Society for Ethical Culture in 1876, said, 'Ethical Culture is religious to those who are religiously minded, and merely ethical to those who are not so minded.' The first British ethical society – the South Place Ethical Society, which exists to this day – was officially established in 1888, having evolved out of a Unitarian church. Numerous other British ethical societies quickly followed.

The various 19th-century ethical societies developed into one of the cornerstones of the modern humanist movement. In 1896, the British ethical societies came together to form the Union of Ethical Societies, retitled in 1967 as the British Humanist Association (BHA). In 1952, the American Ethical Union, an umbrella organization for the various US-based ethical societies, became a founding member of the International Humanist and Ethical Union (IHEU), the organization that now represents the global humanist movement.

The 20th century

In many countries during the second half of the 20th century, humanism became part of the mainstream. In Europe, religious belief went into sharp decline. Surveys indicate, for example, that at the end of the 20th century, about 36% of Britons shared the beliefs and values of humanism and the BHA. Across most of Europe, it is possible to express atheistic or humanistic beliefs without any great fear of the consequences.

Many prominent 20th-century thinkers were humanists, including Bertrand Russell, whose book *Why I Am Not a Christian* was influential. At the end of the 20th century, comparatively few philosophers suppose that morality requires some sort of divine foundation (indeed, a recent poll indicates that only 14.6% of professional philosophers are theists). Today's most prominent and influential ethicist, Peter Singer, is a humanist.

During the 20th century, the kind of religious belief expressed by many theologians and other religious intellectuals has become increasingly difficult to pin down, their religiosity being far more easily characterized in terms of what it isn't than what it is. Indeed, the beliefs of some sophisticated theologians appear scarcely distinguishable from those of some humanists.

Among the world's faithful, however, such 'sophisticated' theological ideas are the exception rather than the rule. Religious fundamentalism is rife. In the United States, polls consistently indicate that about one-third of citizens believe in the literal truth of the Bible and, consequently, that the universe is just a few thousand years old. Atheists are one of the least trusted minorities in the United States, with a national poll indicating atheists are the minority group Americans are least willing to let their children marry. Dorothy Edgell, lead researcher of this University of Minnesota study, said: 'Our findings seem to rest on a view of atheists as self-interested individuals who are not concerned with the common good.' Misconceptions about what humanists believe, and the discrimination they suffer as a result, even within the world's leading liberal democracy, need to be addressed.

Even in many comparatively liberal countries, religious beliefs are given a privileged, state-approved status, and the battle to achieve a level playing field between the religious and non-religious is ongoing. In the United Kingdom, for example, the state funds religious schools that are able to discriminate against both staff and pupils on the basis of their religious beliefs. And every state-funded school in England and Wales is legally required to begin each day with an act of collective worship that is 'wholly or mainly of a broadly Christian character'.

In many countries around the world, to reject the faith into which one was born is to risk social ostracism or worse. Apostate Muslims are executed in Saudi Arabia, Iran, Somalia, Qatar, Yemen, and Mauritania. In Malawi and Nigeria, Christian pastors condemn children for witchcraft who are then beaten, tortured, and sometimes killed in exorcisms. As a result of religious lobbying, Uganda is considering introducing life imprisonment as the minimum sentence for engaging in gay sex. In many parts of the world, religious intolerance is rife, and the fight for even basic rights and freedoms is ongoing.

Both locally and globally, then, there is an enormous number of issues that are of concern, sometimes very grave concern, to humanists – issues on which humanist organizations such as the BHA, CFI, AHA, the European Humanist Federation (EHF), and the IHEU continue to campaign.

Humanists do tend to be reformists. Their views often bring them into conflict with the religious – especially the more conservatively religious – on issues such as birth control, the rights of gays and lesbians, the rights of women, the rights of children, freedom of speech, and an end to religious privilege. This is because what humanists oppose is often (though not always) rooted in religious traditions and institutions and given a religious justification.

However, there are religious people who agree with much or even all of what humanists have to say about such issues – who accept that traditional religious justifications for such discrimination, oppression, and privilege are not tenable – and so humanists can and sometimes do work cooperatively with religious individuals and organizations to achieve shared goals.

It is not, as some religious people suppose, *enmity towards religion* that drives the humanist's reformist ambitions, but rather *a positive commitment to approach moral and political issues rationally and fairly.* Of course, this commitment does inevitably bring humanists into conflict with many religious people on many such issues. But by no means all of them.

It is also worth remembering that humanists are no less opposed to unjust repression and discrimination when carried out by *atheist* regimes, such as those of the 20th-century dictators Mao and Stalin (both of whom were as ruthlessly committed to eradicating Enlightened free-thinkers as they were religious thought).

A brief note on the history of the term 'humanism'

The word 'humanist' was probably first used to describe a branch of the educational curriculum: the *humanities* – comprising grammar, poetry, rhetoric, and moral philosophy. During the Renaissance, there was, as has been noted, a renewed interest in Classical culture and teaching, and an increased focus on the human. This cultural and intellectual movement was subsequently named 'Renaissance humanism' by 19th-century commentators.

Today, the main use of the term 'humanism', both in the UK and around the world, is to describe the sort of position outlined in my introduction. That has been the main meaning of the word for the last 70 years at least – a meaning it began to take on during the 19th century. In the US, some place the word 'secular' before 'humanism' in order to emphasize that their beliefs are divorced from any religious belief. In the UK, the addition of 'secular' is generally considered redundant.

Chapter 2
Arguments for the existence of God

Humanists embrace atheism or agnosticism. They typically suppose that belief in a god or gods is not particularly reasonable or justified. Others go further, insisting that belief in God is actually downright irrational.

Those who believe in God, on the other hand, perhaps even while maintaining their belief is a 'faith position', nevertheless typically suppose their belief is not *un*reasonable. Believing in God, they suppose, is not, say, like believing in Santa or in fairies – it is *much* more reasonable than that. They may well concede that God's existence cannot be conclusively 'proved'. But that God exists, they invariably insist, is at least a *fairly* reasonable thing for a modern, educated adult to believe.

But if believing in God is far more reasonable than, say, believing in fairies, why is this? What makes belief in God more reasonable? Theists – those who believe in God – respond to this question in a variety of ways. Many attempt to offer some sort of *rational argument* for the existence of God.

There are many such arguments. Here I provide illustrations of two of the most popular kinds of argument for God's existence, and indicate where humanist critics believe those arguments fall down. I begin with an example of a cosmological argument, and then move on to some versions of the argument from design, including two contemporary examples based, respectively, on irreducible complexity and fine-tuning. My aim here is merely to provide a brief overview of some of the problems and objections such arguments typically face.

The cosmological argument: why is there anything at all?

Most of us have at some time or other looked up at the starry heavens and been struck by the thought – 'Where did all this come from? Why is there *something*, rather than *nothing*?' This is a profound question – a question worthy of serious consideration.

Scientists have, of course, developed theories about how the universe began. Currently, most scientists believe the universe began roughly 13 or 14 billion years ago with the Big Bang – an event with which not just matter and energy, but time and space, began.

However, such scientific answers appear merely to postpone the mystery rather than to solve it. For, of course, we now want to know – why was there a Big Bang? Why was there – is there – anything at all?

We seem at this point to be faced with a question that, *necessarily*, science cannot answer. Science explains natural phenomena by pointing to other features of the natural world – such as physical causes or the laws of nature. For example, ask a scientist why the water froze in the pipes last night, and they may point out that: (i) it is a law of nature that water freezes below zero degrees Celsius, and (ii) last night the temperature of the water in the pipes fell below zero. That would explain why the water froze. But what explains why there are any laws of nature in the first place? Indeed, what explains why there is a natural world *at all*?

It is at this point, of course, that God is supposed to enter the picture. Science cannot explain why the universe exists, so, unless we suppose its existence is just a brute fact, we must turn to God as the solution to our puzzle. God provides the only, or at least the best available, explanation of why there is anything at all.

While many theists admit that the above argument does not constitute a conclusive proof of God's existence, many believe such 'cosmological' arguments – arguments that infer the existence of God as the best or only explanation of the existence of the universe – do at least lend their belief a good deal of rational support.

Problems with the cosmological argument

The cosmological argument sketched out above runs into several well-known difficulties. I shall outline just three.

First, the argument assumes that the question, 'Why is there something, rather than nothing?' actually makes sense. But does it? On closer examination, that is not so clear. But if the question does not make sense, then it does not require any answer, let alone a religious answer. Below is one line of thought leading to the conclusion that the question is indeed nonsensical.

Often, when we talk about there being 'nothing', we mean there exists, say, an empty bit of space. When I say, 'There's nothing in my cup', I mean that, right now, the space inside my cup is empty. And when I say, 'I am doing nothing right now', I mean that, at this moment in time, I am not engaged in any activity. The spatio-temporal universe supplies, as it were, the stage upon which such examples of something or nothing might appear.

However, when we raise the philosophical question: 'Why is there something, rather than nothing?', we are considering a much more radical sort of nothing – which might be termed *absolute* nothing.

The alternative to something we are now supposed to be envisaging is not merely an absence of stuff or of things going on. We are supposed to be considering this possibility: not only is there no stuff and nothing going on, there's no time or space in which any stuff could exist or anything could go on. The stage itself has now been removed.

This is a profound and baffling sort of absence – so baffling, it is not entirely clear the notion makes sense (it certainly raises some intriguing questions, such as 'What is the difference between thinking about absolute nothing, and not thinking about anything?').

It is tempting to say, 'But of course the notion of absolute nothing makes sense. It's just the notion of *what there used to be*, before anything existed.' But actually, absolute nothing is not what there used to be. There never was a time when there was absolutely nothing (for if there was time, there wasn't absolutely nothing).

However, let's concede, if only for the sake of argument, that the notion of absolute nothing does make sense, and that so too does the question, 'Why is there something rather than nothing?' Our cosmological argument still faces further difficulties.

One obvious difficulty with postulating God as the answer to the question, 'Why is there something, rather than nothing?', as it stands, is that by introducing God, we appear to have introduced just another something, the existence of which now has to be explained. We have, it seems, merely pushed the mystery back a step, rather than to have solved it. If God's existence is left unexplained, what is the justification for introducing God? Why not just stop at the universe itself?

A standard theistic response to this objection is to insist that, unlike the natural universe, God is a *necessary* being – something that cannot but exist.

32

How could something *necessarily* exist? Well, perhaps if the idea of that thing actually involves the idea of existence. We can conceive of the universe not existing. But, some theists argue, we cannot conceive of God not existing. If you conceive of something not existing, it cannot be God you are conceiving of, because the concept of God involves that of existence. In which case, God, if you like, *explains his own existence*. The explanation for God's existence is that *he must, by his very nature, do so*.

But if God is a necessary being, then the search for the ultimate explanation of why there is anything at all comes to a satisfying end – there is no need to look behind God for a further something to account for his existence (and then a further something behind that something that accounts for *its* existence, and so on *ad infinitum*). With God, we reach the end of the line.

However, the notion of necessary existence is by no means uncontroversial. Indeed, many philosophers are sceptical about the claim that something might exist as a matter of necessity.

Take, for example, one leading philosophical view about necessity: that what is essential or necessary is ultimately a product of our linguistic practices and/or ways of conceptualizing things. This is *prima facie* plausible in many cases. For example, isn't the reason it is a necessary condition of something's being a stallion that it be both male and a horse that this is just the *definition* of a stallion? Being both male and a horse are, if you like, built into the concept of a stallion.

But then, on this view of necessity, if God, or something else, exists as a matter of necessity, that can only be *because God is defined or conceptualized that way, as something that exists*.

The problem is: *neither existence nor necessary existence can be conceptually guaranteed in this manner*. If I define 'Woozle' as the person who first walked on the surface of Mars in the year 2000, well then I know that if anyone is Woozle, they were first to walk on Mars in 2000. But, of course, no one walked on Mars in 2000. And note that I cannot guarantee such a person exists simply by adding existence to my definition like so: 'Woozle' is the person who first walked on the surface of Mars in 2000 *and exists*.

Similarly, even if existence were included in the concept of God, that would not entail any such being exists, let alone necessarily exists (which is why those 'ontological' arguments that attempt to prove God exists by pointing out that the concept of God involves that of existence are doomed to fail).

So, *if* the only way a property can attach essentially to something is by our defining or conceptualizing it in a certain manner, but existence cannot be attached in this manner, then *nothing can exist as a matter of necessity*.

Even if the various objections outlined above can all be dealt with, there remain further difficulties with our cosmological argument, including this one: that even if the argument did succeed in establishing the existence of a necessarily existent something-or-other behind the universe, it is, as it stands, a huge and unjustified further leap to the conclusion that this something-or-other is, say, something like a *person*, let alone a person who has moral properties such as supreme goodness, a person who listens to our prayers, who performs miracles, and so on.

Our cosmological argument, as it stands, no more supports belief in, say, the Judaeo-Christian God than it does belief in a supremely powerful and morally ambivalent God, or indeed innumerable other gods and something-or-others. Which, of course, in each case, it barely supports, if at all.

Arguments from design

Let's now turn to the so-called *arguments from design*. These arguments begin with the observation that the natural world, or items within it, appear to have certain remarkable features – such as order and purpose. They conclude that, as God is the only, or at least the best available, explanation of those features, God exists.

Perhaps the best-known argument from design is that presented by William Paley in his *Natural Theology*, published in 1802. Paley argues that, were one to find a complex object such as a watch lying on the ground, it would be unreasonable to suppose that the watch came to exist by chance, or that it had always existed in that form. Given the clear purpose of the watch – to tell the time – and its highly complex construction geared to fulfilling that purpose, it is reasonable to suppose the watch was fashioned by an intelligent being for that purpose. But if that is a very reasonable conclusion to draw in the case of a watch, then surely it is no less reasonable to draw that same conclusion in the case of, say, the human eye, which also has a purpose for which it is exquisitely engineered. That intelligent designer, Paley supposes, is God.

That a biological organ such as the human eye must have some sort of designer was accepted by very many, including even the scientist Charles Darwin, up until Darwin developed his own alternative evolutionary account of how the eye appeared.

The mechanism Darwin realized could account for the gradual evolution of the eye is *natural selection*. When living organisms reproduce, their offspring may differ slightly in inheritable ways. Plant and animal breeders take advantage of these chance mutations to breed new strains. For example, a dog breeder might select from each generation of dogs those that are the largest and least hairy, eventually producing a whole new breed of huge, bald dog.

Darwin's great insight was to recognize that the natural environment in which organisms are located will, in effect, also select among offspring. Organisms with a chance mutation that enhances their ability to survive and reproduce in that environment will be more likely to pass that mutation on. Organisms with a mutation that reduces their chances of surviving and reproducing in that environment will be less likely to pass it on. And so, over many generations, organisms will gradually adapt to their environments. Indeed, under certain conditions, a whole new species may emerge.

Darwin called this mechanism 'natural selection', contrasting it with the kind of artificial selection used by dog and plant breeders. Unlike artificial selection, natural selection does not require an intelligent mind to guide the selection process towards a particular end. Selection is now taken care of entirely by blind, unthinking nature.

There is overwhelming fossil and other evidence both that the human eye did, indeed, evolve gradually over millions of years, beginning perhaps with the chance appearance of a single light-sensitive cell in an organism living many millions of years ago, and that natural selection is the main mechanism that drove this evolutionary process.

The discovery of the mechanism of natural selection led Darwin to reject Paley's argument from design. Darwin wrote:

> The old argument of design in nature, as given by Paley, which formerly seemed to me so conclusive, fails, now that the law of natural selection has been discovered.

While the development of Darwin's theory of natural selection, and, later, the theory of genetics, resulted in a decline in the popularity of arguments from design, such arguments have recently been making something of a come-back. Two popular, more recent variants of the argument from design are outlined below.

The argument from irreducible complexity

Some, such as Professor of Biochemistry Michael Behe, author of *Darwin's Black Box*, argue that there are certain features of biological organisms that Darwin's theory of natural selection cannot explain. While Behe accepts both that new species evolve and that natural selection plays a role in this, he maintains that *some* biological systems are *irreducibly complex*, and so cannot have evolved by natural selection.

By an irreducibly complex system, Behe means:

> a single system composed of several well-matched, interacting parts that contribute to the basic function, wherein the removal of any one of the parts causes the system to effectively cease functioning.

Behe uses the mousetrap to illustrate. Take any one part away – the base, the spring, the cheese – and the entire mechanism fails to function. According to Behe,

> an irreducibly complex biological system, if there is such a thing, would be a powerful challenge to Darwinian evolution.

It seems there are irreducibly complex systems in nature. Behe provides a number of illustrations, including a certain sort of bacterial flagellum – a whip-like appendage bacteria use to propel themselves. Each flagellum has at its base a kind of molecular motor drive comprising several components, each of which is essential if the flagellum is to work.

Why does Behe suppose that an irreducibly complex system such as this flagellum cannot evolve gradually by natural selection? Because, thinks Behe, *there can be no reproductive or survival value to having only a part of the system*. Remove any component and the result is useless junk. So the system

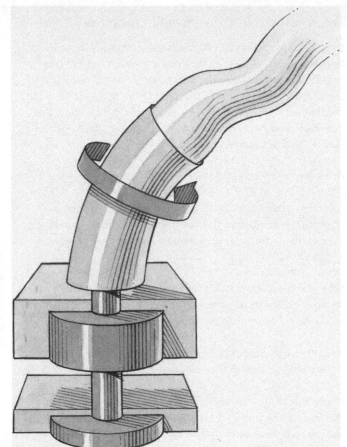

4. The base of a bacterial flagellum (this image exaggerates its 'engineered' appearance)

cannot evolve by stages. And the probability of the entire system spontaneously appearing in a single generation as a result of chance mutation is so low that it is far more reasonable to suppose some sort of intelligent designer lent a helping hand.

Behe's argument for intelligent design is popular in certain religious circles. Some maintain that because the scientific community is supposedly divided on the question of whether some intelligence played a role in the emergence of life, the theory of intelligent design should be taught in schools alongside the theories of evolution and natural selection. This suggestion is designed to appeal to our sense of fairness – surely it *is* only fair that both sides in a scientific controversy should get a hearing?

The truth, however, is that the 'scientific controversy' about intelligent design is a myth. There is no scientific controversy. Behe's arguments have been entirely scientifically discredited.

In fact, there are plausible natural mechanisms for all of Behe's examples of irreducibly complex systems. As Professor of Biology Kenneth R. Miller points out, one of the ways in which natural selection can produce irreducibly complex systems is by combining elements that have previously evolved by natural selection to perform *other* functions. Just because a part of the flagellum would, by itself, be useless for propelling the organism around does not entail that the part is non-functional. Indeed, we know that some of the components of the bacterial flagellum do have functions elsewhere:

> [Behe] writes that in the absence of 'almost any' of its parts, the bacterial flagellum 'does not work.' But guess what? A small group of proteins from the flagellum does work without the rest of the machine — it's used by many bacteria as a device for injecting poisons into other cells. Although the function performed by this small part when working alone is different, it nonetheless can be favored by natural selection.

In short, Behe's key claim that possessing only *part* of an irreducibly complex mechanism can have no reproductive or survival value for the organism is simply false. If you suspect that Miller says this because he is an atheist dogmatically committed to rejecting any form of intelligent design, think again: Miller is religious. It is not, says Miller, anti-religious bias that explains why the scientific community rejects Behe's arguments:

> In the final analysis, the biochemical hypothesis of intelligent design fails not because the scientific community is closed to it but rather for the most basic of reasons — because it is overwhelmingly contradicted by the scientific evidence.

The physicist Lawrence Krauss writes:

> The dishonesty of [intelligent design] lies in its proponents pointing to a controversy when there really is no controversy. A friend of mine did an informal survey of more than ten million articles in major science journals during the past twelve years. Searching for the key word evolution pulled up 115,000 articles, most pertaining to biological evolution. Searching for Intelligent Design yielded eighty-eight articles. All but eleven of those were in engineering journals, where, of course, we hope there is discussion of intelligent design! Of the eleven articles, eight were critical of the scientific basis for Intelligent Design theory and the remaining three turned out to be articles in conference proceedings, not peer-reviewed research journals. So that's the extent of the 'controversy' in the scientific literature. There is none.

To teach children that there is a 'scientific controversy' about intelligent design is to teach them a falsehood. There may indeed be a controversy, but it is not a *scientific* controversy.

The fine-tuning argument

According to certain current theories of physics, our universe appears to be 'fine-tuned' for life. It is suggested that for life to emerge, the laws of nature and initial conditions of the universe have to be just right. Had certain forces been slightly stronger or weaker, or certain dimensions or values slightly smaller or larger, life either could not, or would have been very unlikely to, appear. Here, for example, is Stephen Hawking:

> The remarkable fact is that the values of these [fundamental] numbers seem to have been very finely adjusted to make possible the development of life. For example, if the electric charge of the electron had been only slightly different, stars either would have been unable to burn hydrogen and helium, or they would have exploded.

It is often said that the probability of the universe having such a combination of features just by chance is very small indeed. So small, in fact, that some believe it more reasonable to suppose that some sort of intelligent agent deliberately *designed* the universe this way. This intelligence, many will add, is God. God supplies a satisfying explanation for what would otherwise be an extraordinarily improbable set of coincidences. It is therefore reasonable to believe God exists.

To what extent do these and other observations of the natural world really support belief in God? Hardly, if at all.

To begin with, note that the scientific claims on which the fine-tuning argument is based are not entirely uncontroversial.

A number of scientists question whether there is only a very narrow range of physical parameters within which life can emerge. Physicists including Victor Stenger, Anthony Aguire, and Craig Hogan have studied those universes that result when six cosmological parameters are simultaneously varied by several orders of magnitude, and have found that stars, planets, and intelligent life can plausibly arise within many of them. According to these physicists, it is by no means obvious that there is only a very narrow set of physical parameters within which life might arise. If they are correct, the universe is not fine-tuned.

Other scientists believe that, while the universe is fine-tuned, there may well be a multiverse – a plethora of universes governed by a wide range of different physical laws. If there is a multiverse, then it's not particularly unlikely that there should happen to exist a universe that is fine-tuned: that has the Goldilocks property of being 'just right' for life.

But still, let's concede, for the sake of argument, that the science on which cosmic fine-tuning arguments are based has been established beyond reasonable doubt. Let's suppose both that the universe is fine-tuned and that there is no multiverse.

There are many more problems with the fine-tuning argument. A key idea on which such arguments rely – that we can talk intelligibly about the universe and its basic features as being either 'probable' or 'improbable' – has also repeatedly been challenged by philosophers (some argue, for example, that the notion of probability being applied here can only be applied relative to a particular set of physical laws and conditions, which, of course, can only obtain *within* a physical universe).

Still, let's suppose, for the sake of argument, both that the universe is significantly fine-tuned for life, and also that it is highly improbable it should have such life-supporting features just by chance. To what extent would this fact support belief in the existence of some sort of transcendent, intelligent being who deliberately designed our universe that way?

A further objection to the fine-tuning argument – made by Richard Dawkins and others – is that by appealing to a cosmic intelligent designer, we are appealing to a being who must be at least as complex, and so at least as improbable, as the universe he is supposed to have designed. If the complexity of the universe should lead us to suppose it has a designer, shouldn't the complexity of the designer lead us to suppose that designer had a designer, and so on *ad infinitum*?

Does the transcendent intelligence hypothesis even make sense?

But even if we also set this objection to one side, there remain at least two further, perhaps deeper, difficulties – difficulties that threaten all arguments from design.

The first difficulty is that it is by no means obvious that the idea of a transcendent intelligent designer makes sense.

Human beings explain features of the world around them in two main ways. One way is to supply *naturalistic* explanations that appeal to features of the natural world, such as natural events, forces, and laws. The explanations of physics and chemistry fall into this category. The other is to offer *intentional* explanations – explanations that appeal to the beliefs and desires of more or less rational agents. Why is there a tree in this spot? Because Ted wanted to see a tree from his bedroom window, and so planted a sapling here correctly supposing it would grow into a handsome oak.

When we are unable to explain something naturalistically, it is, of course, tempting to look for an intentional explanation instead. When we could not offer naturalistic explanations for why the heavenly bodies moved about as they did, we supposed that they must be, or must be moved by, agents – gods of some sort. When we could not otherwise explain diseases and natural disasters, we put them down to the actions of malevolent agents, such as witches and demons. When we could not provide naturalistic explanations for the growth of plants and the cycle of the seasons, we again invoked agents – sprites, fairies, and gods of various sorts.

As our scientific understanding of the world has increased, so the need to invoke witches, fairies, demons, and other supernatural agents to account for features of the natural world has diminished.

However, when we ask: 'Why does the natural world exist at all, and what explains why it has the fundamental laws it does?', such naturalistic explanations are unavailable. So an explanation in terms of the activity of some sort of transcendent agent might seem attractive, even inevitable.

But does such an explanation make sense? Suppose I claim that there exists a non-spatial mountain. It's a mountain – with a sharp summit flanked by steep valleys and crags. Only this mountain is not located or extended in space at all. It does not have spatial dimensions. The mountain transcends our spatial world.

You might well ask why I suppose there is any such mountain. And if I cannot give you good reasons, you will rightly be sceptical. But actually, isn't there a rather more fundamental problem with my claim that such a mountain exists? Can't we know, even before we get to the question of whether there is any *evidence* for or against the existence of my mountain, that there can be no such thing? For the very idea of a non-spatial mountain makes no sense. My hypothetical mountain has a summit, valleys, and cliffs, but these are all features that require spatial extension. A summit requires that one part of the mountain be higher than another. A valley must be lower than the surrounding terrain. The concepts of a mountain, a summit, and so on are concepts that can only sensibly be applied within a spatial context. Strip that context away and we end up talking nonsense.

But if we now turn to the concept of a transcendent designer, does that make any more sense? The concept of an agent has its home within a temporal setting. The concept of an agent is the concept of someone or something with *beliefs* and *desires* on which they might more or less rationally *act*. But actions are events that happen at particular moments in time. And beliefs and desires are psychological states that have temporal duration.

44

Now, when we suppose that the spatio-temporal universe was created by God, we are presumably supposing it was created by a non-temporal agent – an agent that does not (or at least did not then) exist in time. For, of course, there was not yet any time for the agent to exist in. But if desires are psychological states with temporal duration, how could this agent possess the desire to create the universe? And how did it perform the act of creation if there was not yet any time in which actions might be performed? It is hard to see how talk of a non-temporal agent makes any more sense than talk of a non-spatial mountain.

We might sidestep these puzzles by supposing that God exists, and has always existed, in time. This provides God with the necessary temporal setting in which he might possess the desire to produce a universe, draw up a design, and perform the act of creation. But it throws up a host of other baffling questions, such as: why did it take God so long to get round to creating the universe (presumably, an infinitely long time)? Did he always have the desire to create such a universe – if so, why did he wait so long before acting on it (and what was he doing in the meantime)? Or, if he was acting on a newly formed desire, why did this new desire spontaneously arise in him? (Indeed, how could any new desire arise if God is supposed to be *changeless*: 'I am the Lord, I do not change' [Malachi 3.6].)

Alternatively, we might, as many theists do, insist that talk of an intelligent designer should not be understood literally. We are positing not a *literal* intelligent agent, but something merely *analogous to* such an agent.

Does this appeal to analogy succeed in salvaging explanation in terms of intelligent design? Suppose I try to explain some natural phenomenon by appealing to the existence of a non-spatial mountain. My critics point out that the notion of such a mountain makes no sense. I roll my eyes and insist they are interpreting me in far too crude and literal a manner. I am not talking about a *literal* mountain – oh no – but about something that is merely *analogous to* a mountain. Does that salvage my explanation?

Suppose my analogy is this: that the guilt of a nation concerning some terrible deed it performed is like a vast mountain weighing down on the collective psyche of its citizens. That's certainly a nice analogy we might develop in various ways. Now suppose the country in question experiences a severe earthquake. I try to explain the earthquake by appealing to this something-merely-analogous-to-a-mountain. Clearly, that *wouldn't* explain the earthquake. Something merely *analogous to* a mountain does not possess the same causal and explanatory powers as a real mountain. Collective guilt can't cause earthquakes.

You can now see why those who try to explain features of the universe by appealing to something merely *analogous to* an intelligent agent have, at the very least, a lot of explaining to do. They have a duty clearly to explain: (i) precisely what the intended analogy is, (ii) how their analogy is supposed to avoid the charge of nonsense levelled at the literally understood version of the claim, and also (iii) how this something-that-is-merely-analogous-to-an-intelligent-agent is nevertheless supposed to retain the relevant explanatory powers possessed by a real intelligent agent.

Can those who appeal to something merely *analogous to* an intelligent agent provide these explanations? It is not clear to me that they can (often, they don't even bother to try). Such appeals to analogy seem to many commentators, myself included, to bring the debate about intelligent design, not up to a level of great sophistication and profundity, but down to the level of evasion and obfuscation.

Why a *god*? And why *that* God?

Even if we set all these various objections to one side, there remains what is possibly the most damning of all. Which is that it is a huge and, as it stands, unjustified leap from the conclusion that the universe is the product of an intelligence to the conclusion that this intelligence is, say, the all-powerful and limitlessly benevolent God of love worshiped by Christians, Muslims, or Jews.

As the Templeton-prize-winning physicist Paul Davies points out at the end of his book *The Goldilocks Enigma*, even putting aside all the other difficulties:

> The other main problem with intelligent design is that identity of the designer need bear no relation at all to the God of traditional monotheism. The 'designing agency' can be a committee of gods, for example. The designer can be a natural being or beings, such as an evolved super-mind or super-civilization existing in a previous universe, or in another section of our universe, which made our universe using super-technology. The designer can also be some sort of superdupercomputer simulating this universe. So invoking a super-intellect . . . is fraught with problems.

Davies is correct, of course. That even if certain features of the universe did point towards a designer, they no more point towards the existence of the Christian God than they point towards the universe being a computer-generated simulation, or the creation of an earlier super-civilization, or, of course, to some other sort of god.

Why a *god*? And why *that* God? We have not, as yet, been provided with answers to these questions.

Conclusion

In this chapter, we have looked at examples of two kinds of argument widely considered to provide belief in God with a fair degree of rational support: cosmological arguments and arguments from design. On closer examination, the arguments examined turned out to support, at the very most, only the claim that there exists some sort of intelligence, or perhaps a necessarily-existing-something-or-other, behind the universe (and I believe we have seen good reason to suppose they fail to achieve even this much). It is, in each case, on the basis of the argument presented, a huge and unjustified further leap to the conclusion that this intelligence is, say, the God of traditional monotheism.

Chapter 3
An argument against the existence of God

The previous chapter focused on arguments *for* the existence of God. In this chapter, we turn to an argument *against* the existence of God.

The problems of evil

God, as traditionally conceived by the three monotheistic faiths of Judaism, Christianity, and Islam, has at least three important characteristics. First, God is omnipotent or maximally powerful. God has the ability to create the universe and destroy it again. Being the creator and sustainer of the laws of nature, he is also free to break them by, for example, raising people from the dead or parting the Red Sea. Second, God is omniscient. His knowledge is unlimited. He knows even our most private thoughts. Third, God is supposed to be supremely benevolent. Indeed, God is often characterized as watching over us as a loving parent watches over his children. God, it is said, is love.

I shall use the term 'Theist' with a capital 'T' to refer to those who believe in such a being, and 'God' with a capital G as the name of that being. Small initial 'theists', by contrast, are those who believe in a god or gods, whether or not it happens to be God.

If God has the three characteristics of omnipotence, omniscience, and supreme benevolence, this raises an obvious and familiar challenge to Theism, a challenge known as the *problem of evil*. In fact, there are at least two problems of evil: the logical problem and the evidential problem.

The logical problem of evil

The *logical problem of evil* begins with the thought that the claim:

1) There exists an omnipotent, omniscient, and maximally good God

is logically inconsistent with the claim:

2) Evil exists.

By 'evil', here, we mean both suffering and morally wrong actions. The argument runs like so: (2) is true, therefore (1) is false. Why? Because an omnipotent God would have the power to prevent evil, an omniscient God would know it exists, and a supremely benevolent God would want to prevent it.

Note that the quantity of evil that exists is irrelevant to the above argument. It requires only that there exist *some*, no matter how little.

Many Theists maintain the logical problem of evil does not present an insuperable challenge to belief in God. In response, they typically try to show that an all-powerful, all-knowing, and maximally good God might allow some evil for the sake of a greater good.

For example, many Theists believe God gave us free will – the ability freely to choose to do good or evil. As a result of our acting freely, evil exists. However, this evil is more than outweighed by other goods that free will brings, such as the ability to perform good deeds of our own volition. So, though it might sound paradoxical, this is actually a better world than one lacking free will, despite the fact that, as a result of free will, there exists, say, war and murder.

Note that the free will defence does not (typically) address the problem of natural evil, that is, the suffering that arises independently of actions by humans, such as that caused by naturally occurring diseases and disasters. Why does such evil exist? As we will see, Theists often offer a similar response, namely that natural evil is necessary for some greater good, such as consistency in the laws of nature or the opportunity for humans to display virtues such as fortitude and courage in the face of calamities.

The evidential problem of evil

There is, however, another, to my mind far more serious, problem of evil facing Theism – the *evidential* problem of evil. The evidential problem rests, not on the thought that the truth of (2) *logically entails* the falsity of (1), but on the thought that (2) provides us with *good evidence* against (1).

The quantity of evil does now become relevant. While we might concede that God might allow *some* evil (for the sake of a greater good), surely there could be no good reason for God to allow quite so much? We can sharpen the evidential problem by noting that God will presumably not allow *gratuitous* suffering to exist. Presumably, if God exists, he must have good reason to allow every last ounce of it.

At the end of a recent episode of the television programme *Life*, one of the cameramen was interviewed. He revealed that, after just a few weeks on the job, he was already considering giving up wildlife photography because he found the experience too harrowing. He was struggling to cope with the extraordinary degree of suffering endured by the creatures he was observing. That kind of suffering – appalling suffering, on a vast, global scale – has of course been going on, not just for a few weeks, but for many hundreds of millions of years, long before we humans made our comparatively very recent appearance.

When we begin to consider the enormous quantities of suffering that exist – including the hundreds of millions of years of animal suffering that occurred before we humans showed up – doesn't it quickly become apparent that it cannot all be accounted for by the suggestion that it serves some greater good?

It might seem, then, that the claim that the God of classical monotheism exists is straightforwardly empirically falsified.

Theodicies

Those who believe in God respond to the evidential problem of evil in a variety of ways. Some maintain there are good grounds for supposing that, not only is there a god, this being does indeed have the properties attributed to him by traditional monotheism. So, while there may be evidence against the existence of God, it is at least counter-balanced by supporting arguments. I return to that suggestion later in this chapter. Theists may also insist that the evidential problem of evil can, to a significant extent, be dealt with. Many Theistic explanations of evil have been offered, including the following three examples:

> *Simple free will solution.* God created us as free agents with the ability to choose how to act. Suffering results from our choosing to do things that are wrong. However, free will also allows for certain important goods, such as the ability to do good of our own volition. Puppet creatures that always did as God commands would not do evil. But such puppet beings lack moral responsibility, and so are unable to act in a genuinely virtuous manner. By cutting our strings and setting us free, God inevitably allowed some evil (such as that

done by Hitler). But the good free will allows more than outweighs those evils.

Second-order goods require first-order evils. God had inevitably to create a certain amount of suffering so that certain important goods could obtain. Take charity, for example. In order for me to be charitable, I must suppose there are others who are in need, and who might benefit from my generosity. Charity is a *second-order good* that requires *first-order evils* like neediness and suffering (or at least their appearance) to exist. It is because the second-order goods outweigh the first-order evils that God permits them.

The 'character-building' solution. According to the theologian John Hick, this world is a 'vale of soul making'. We are all familiar with the idea that suffering can make us stronger, better people. For example, someone who has suffered a serious and painful illness will sometimes say they don't regret it, because they learnt so much from the experience. By causing us pain and suffering, God furnishes us with important opportunities, including the opportunity to learn and to grow and develop morally and spiritually. It is only by means of such suffering that we can become the kind of noble souls God intends.

When offered in response to the evidential problem of evil, such explanations are sometimes called *theodicies*. Many have been developed. Some Theists believe that, even if the evidential problem of evil has not been entirely solved, such theodicies collectively bring the problem down to at least a manageable size, so that we can no longer say that Theism has been straightforwardly empirically falsified.

Still, those who believe in God will often acknowledge that it certainly isn't easy to explain why God would inflict quite so much pain and suffering on the sentient inhabitants of this planet. So some supplement these various explanations with a further appeal – to *mystery*. God, they insist, works in mysterious ways. God is infinitely knowledgeable and intelligent, his divine plan is likely to be mostly 'beyond our ken'. So the fact that the reason for much of the evil that exists is beyond our understanding is not good evidence that there is no God.

The evil god hypothesis

Of course, most atheists consider these various explanations for moral catastrophes and natural disasters fairly hopeless. It seems to many that the sheer quantity of suffering and moral depravity that exists does constitute excellent evidence that there is no such God. Indeed, to many, it appears fairly obvious that there is no God.

Could it be fairly obvious that there is no God, even given the appeal to mystery and the various theodicies and other strategies Theists have developed to defend their belief? My personal view is that, yes, it could.

Consider a rather different belief: that the universe was designed and created by an omnipotent, omniscient being. Only this being is not all-good. Rather, he is supremely evil. His cruelty and malice know no bounds.

Note that I am considering this alternative god hypothesis, not because I think that it is likely to be true, but to raise the question: is it actually any less plausible than the good god hypothesis?

Of course, almost everyone considers the evil god hypothesis absurd. Why? Well, there is, for a start, a great deal of evidence against it. Surely, an all-powerful, all-knowing, and all-evil being would not allow quite so many good things into his creation. Why, for example, would such an evil being:

- Create natural beauty that gives us so much joy?

- Give us children to love who love us unconditionally in return. Evil god despises love, and so is hardly likely to introduce such bundles of joy into his creation.

- Give us healthy bodies so that we can enjoy sports, sex, and so on?

- Allow us to help each other and alleviate each other's suffering. That, surely, is not the sort of behaviour an evil god would tolerate. He would compel us to cause greater suffering, rather than allow us to reduce it.

- Bestow upon at least some people immense health, wealth, and happiness?

Don't these observable features of the universe provide us with overwhelming evidence against the evil god hypothesis? Indeed, isn't it fairly obvious that there is no such being, given the evidence? We might call this problem facing the evil god hypothesis the *evidential problem of good*.

But perhaps we have been too hasty in rejecting belief in an evil god. Notice that we might try to defend the evil god hypothesis by developing explanations such as these:

Simple free will solution. Evil god created us as free agents with the ability to choose how to act. Many goods results from our choosing to do things that are right. So why did evil god create free will? Because it allows for certain important evils, such as the ability to do evil of our own volition. Puppet creatures that always did as evil god commanded might inflict pain and suffering on each other. But they would lack moral responsibility, and so be unable to act in a genuinely morally evil manner. By cutting our strings and setting us free, evil god inevitably allowed some good. But the evil free will allows more than outweighs those goods.

Second-order evils require first-order goods. Theists may remind us that God had inevitably to create a reasonable amount of good in order that certain important evils could exist. Take, for example, jealousy. Jealousy is an important vice, but it can only exist if there exist people who have good things worth coveting – such as health, wealth, and happiness. Jealousy is a so-called *second-order evil* that requires certain *first-order goods*. It is because the second-order evil outweighs the first-order goods that God allows those goods to exist.

The 'character-destroying' solution. This is a vale of soul destruction. Why does evil god pepper our world with beauty? To make the dreariness and ugliness of day-to-day life seem all the more acute. Why does he give us healthy young bodies? Well, yes, he gives us them for a short time, and then slowly and inexorably takes our health and vitality away, until we end up incontinent, arthritic, and decrepit. It is so much more cruel to give someone something wonderful and then take it from them than never to have given it to them at all. And of course, evil god makes sure that even while we enjoy good health, we are filled with anxiety knowing it could all be snatched away by a disease or accident. Why does he give us children whom we love more than life itself? Because this allows evil god to inflict greater tortures on us. We can only be made to agonize about our children because we care about them. The more we care, the more we can be made to suffer.

Notice these explanations can be supplemented by a further manoeuvre – an appeal to *mystery*. Evil god works in mysterious ways. Being infinitely knowledgeable and intelligent, God's diabolical plan is likely to be mostly 'beyond our ken'. So the fact that the reason for the good that exists lies largely beyond our understanding is not good evidence that there's no such malignant being.

The evil god challenge

You will have noticed some obvious symmetries between the good and evil god hypotheses. These who believe in a good God face the evidential problem of evil. Those who believe in an evil god face the evidential problem of good. Those who believe in a good God may try to deal with the problem of evil by constructing theodicies, such as the free-will and character-building theodicies, and by appealing to mystery. Similarly, those who believe in an evil god may construct mirror theodicies, and also appeal to mystery, in order to deal with the problem of good. Indeed, mirror theodicies can also be constructed for most other theodicies as well.

How reasonable is belief in an evil god, compared to belief in the God of traditional monotheism? Almost everyone recognizes that, even given the ingenious defensive manoeuvres of the sort developed above, belief in a supremely evil deity remains absurd. I suppose it is *possible* that such a being exists. But surely it is overwhelmingly unlikely, given the available evidence.

But if that is true, why should we consider belief in an all-powerful, all-knowing, and all-good God significantly more reasonable? If the sheer quantity of good we observe in the world really is excellent evidence that there is no evil god, why isn't the sheer quantity of evil excellent evidence that there is no God?

So those who believe in the god of traditional monotheism face a challenge. In the previous chapter, we saw that some of the most important and popular arguments widely supposed to provide belief in God with at least a fair degree of rational support actually provide no more support for belief in a good God than they do, say, an evil god. We have seen that the problem of good does appear to provide overwhelming empirical evidence against the evil god hypothesis, notwithstanding the various mirror theodicies and the appeal to mystery that might be made in its defence. But then, if those who believe in a good God consider their belief to be, if not 'proved' then at least not *un*reasonable, the onus is surely now on them to explain *why* their belief should be considered significantly more reasonable than belief in an evil god. We might call this *the evil god challenge*.

I don't claim this challenge cannot be met. However, I cannot see how it can be met, which is why I personally consider belief in the God of traditional monotheism to be hardly more reasonable than belief in an evil god, the latter, surely, being very unreasonable indeed.

Miracles and religious experience

Let's briefly consider some suggestions as to how this challenge to the rationality of Theism might be met. One fairly obvious strategy would be to try to provide arguments for supposing that not only is there a creator god, but also that this being is good. While the arguments from design discussed in the previous chapter may not support the good god hypothesis any more than they do the evil god hypothesis, perhaps *other* arguments do clearly favour the good god hypothesis?

Obvious candidates are the arguments from miracles and from religious experience. People regularly pray that someone should be cured of an otherwise incurable disease, and occasionally these prayers are answered. God supernaturally intervenes to perform a miracle. Isn't such supernatural activity good evidence of the existence of a benevolent, not malevolent, god? Moreover, when people report religious experiences, they generally report a very positive episode, such as an experience of something immeasurably loving and good. Again, doesn't this provide us with at least some evidence that there exists not just a god, but God?

I am not so sure. If I were an evil god, I would not necessarily want people to know I was evil, particularly if, by pretending to be good, I could actually produce more evil.

For example, were I an evil god, I might appear to two different populations in a 'good' guise and perform supernatural miracles to convince each that I was real. If I then tell one group things that contradict what I tell the other, the result is entirely predictable: endless conflict of a particularly vicious sort, given each population now possesses 'proof' that the one true God is on their side, and that their opponents are deniers of His Truth.

So are religious miracles and experiences better evidence of a good God than an evil god? Surely, a good God, knowing the horrendous moral catastrophes that would result if he were to reveal himself in this way, will avoid doing so. He will ensure there is no such confusion about who has God on their side and what people should believe. An evil god, by contrast, might well calculate that revealing himself in such a deceptive and confusing manner would create a situation in which evil is likely to flourish. So it is not clear that religious experiences and miracles are better evidence of a good God than an evil god. Indeed, we might argue that the actual distribution of these phenomena fits the evil god hypothesis rather better than it fits the good.

Other theodicies

Are there other theodicies more successful in defending Theism, theodicies that cannot, perhaps, be mirrored? Other standard theodicies that can be mirrored include, for example:

> *Semantic theodicy.* The terms 'good' and 'evil', when applied to God, mean something other than what they mean when applied to mere human beings. God, being a transcendent being, cannot adequately be characterized in such human terms. This explains why an action that would be deemed evil if performed by a human (such as inflicting great suffering on an innocent person) need not be evil if performed by God.

It takes but a moment's thought to realize that much the same manoeuvre can be used to explain why an evil god would do things that, if done by a human, would be deemed 'good'.

It is also possible to mirror, for example, those theodicies that explain natural evils (such as earthquakes and diseases) as

5. Adam and Eve chose to sin (though, not yet knowing good and evil, how could they sin?)

resulting from laws of nature that, on balance, produce more good than evil, and also those theodicies that claim any evils endured in this world are more than compensated for in the next life (I'll leave you to figure out the details for yourself).

However, I suspect that at least one standard theodicy cannot easily be mirrored. St Augustine tried to explain the natural evils by supposing that they are a result of the Fall. Adam and Eve inhabited a perfect world untroubled by natural disasters and disease; when they disobeyed God and sinned, they corrupted not only themselves, but nature too. Disease, natural disasters, and death are results of this corruption. So these evils are, in effect, results of free will. Adam and Eve freely chose to sin, and so do we. As a result, we suffer terribly. That suffering would cease if only we would stop sinning and commit ourselves to God.

It is not clear to me that a mirror version of this Augustinian theodicy can be produced. Attempts to construct an even vaguely coherent reverse story about a reverse Adam and Eve, who, by disobeying their evil creator, bring about a reverse Fall, thereby creating natural goods, runs into all sorts of difficulties. Perhaps a rather different narrative involving an evil god might account for natural goods, but it is hard to see how it could mirror the story of the Fall in sufficient detail to qualify as a reverse theodicy.

So perhaps not *every* standard theodicy designed to defend belief in a good God can be flipped round to produce a reverse theodicy that might be used to defend belief in an evil god.

However, while Augustine's theodicy appears not to be reversible, it is particularly weak. Adam and Eve never existed. But then their sin cannot explain contemporary natural disasters. Nor can earthquakes be explained as a consequence of our own sin. Earthquakes are produced by the movement of tectonic plates which, given the laws of nature, are going to cause earthquakes anyway, whether we sin or not. And of course, we know that earthquakes, tidal waves, volcanic eruptions, diseases, and so on were occurring for millions of years before moral agents capable of sin existed. How, then, can the immense suffering these events cause be a result of sin or of some kind of 'Fall'?

Evidential problem of evil: conclusion

We have been looking at the evidential problem of evil – which constitutes perhaps the most powerful argument against traditional monotheism. The particular version of the problem of evil presented here, which involves drawing a parallel with the problem of good, has been developed by a number of philosophers, including Peter Millican, Steven Cahn, and myself. My aim here has been to illustrate just how serious a threat this version of the evidential problem constitutes to the rationality of Theism.

Notice that my focus here has been on God with a capital 'G'. The problem of evil may constitute powerful evidence against a good God, and the problem of good, powerful evidence against an evil god, but there are many other god hypotheses we might consider, none of which are threatened by these particular arguments. I don't happen to believe there exists, for example, an omnipotent but morally neutral god. But at least that particular god hypothesis does not run

6. 'I cannot persuade myself that a beneficent and omnipotent god would have designed parasitic wasps with the express intention of feeding within the living bodies of caterpillars', Charles Darwin

up against the kind of evidence that appears straightforwardly to falsify both the evil god and good God hypotheses.

Notice that the evil god challenge constitutes a threat not just to Theism but also to *agnosticism* regarding God. Surely, agnosticism is not a reasonable position to adopt regarding an evil god? It is clear, given the evidence, that there is no such supremely malignant being. But if agnosticism is not reasonable with regard to the evil god hypothesis, why should we consider agnosticism any more reasonable with respect to the good God hypothesis?

'Surely it cannot be *fairly obvious* there is no God?'

Of course, the suggestion that it might be fairly obvious that the God of traditional monotheism does not exist (perhaps even as obvious as that there is no evil god) will strike many – including even some atheists – as odd. How can it be fairly obvious that there is no God if many millions of people – many of them smart, sophisticated people – believe in God nevertheless?

But of course, religion has an extraordinary track record of getting even intelligent, well-educated people to believe things that are obviously false. For example, polls consistently indicate that, currently, about one hundred million US citizens, many of whom are reasonably well educated – some college educated – believe that the entire universe is only about 6,000 years old. For anyone with a decent level of education, it should, surely, be pretty obvious that the universe is a lot older than that. Other bright, otherwise sophisticated people believe all sorts of patently absurd things because that is what their religion teaches them (consider those scientologists who believe an alien ruler brought billions of people to Earth in spacecraft shaped like Douglas DC-10 aeroplanes and stacked them around volcanoes which he then blew up with hydrogen bombs).

When it comes to religion, the fact that many bright and learned people believe something is not particularly good evidence that what they believe is not, in fact, fairly obviously false.

'I may not be able to *prove* there is a God, but no one can *prove* that there isn't'

When presented with a rational challenge to their belief, Theists sometimes say, 'Look, I cannot *prove* there is a God; but then it is not possible to *prove* that there isn't. So Theism and atheism are both "faith positions". But then it follows that they are *equally* reasonable or unreasonable.'

But what, exactly, does 'prove' mean here? Prove beyond all *possible* doubt? It may well be true that we cannot prove beyond all possible doubt that there is no God. But then we cannot prove beyond all possible doubt that there are no fairies or unicorns or Santa. It's just possible these things exist (perhaps there has been a huge and elaborate CIA-led conspiracy to hide the truth from us). But of course, no one insists that belief in the non-existence of Santa is, then, a 'faith position'. Certainly, it does not follow that belief in Santa is just as reasonable as belief that there is no Santa.

Perhaps the suggestion is that it is not possible to prove beyond *reasonable* doubt that God does or does not exist? But that is a very contentious suggestion. Actually, many Theists believe that the existence of God can be established beyond reasonable doubt. And almost everyone accepts that the available evidence establishes beyond reasonable doubt that there is no evil god. But surely, anyone who acknowledges that ought, then, to acknowledge at least the *possibility* of there being evidence sufficient to establish beyond reasonable doubt that there is no good God either.

'So how do atheists explain...?'

If we reject belief in God, how do we respond to one of the questions with which we began Chapter 2 – why does the universe exist? What is our answer? Personally, I am not at all sure about how to answer this question. This is a deep and baffling puzzle to which I am not confident I possess a satisfactory solution.

Some Theists may take this to be an astonishing admission: 'If you do not know the answer, then you do not know that our answer is incorrect! Your view is no less a faith position than ours.'

But to admit that one does not know the answer to a question is not to say that certain answers cannot reasonably be ruled out. Suppose Sherlock Holmes is having a bad day. There's been a terrible murder. There are hundreds of suspects. And Holmes just can't figure out who dunnit. However, while Holmes can't identify who the culprit is, he is quite sure that certain people are innocent. The butler, in particular, has a cast-iron alibi. So Holmes is justifiably confident the butler didn't do it, despite the fact that he doesn't know who did.

In the same way, atheists can admit that there is a mystery about why the universe exists, and that they are utterly baffled by it, while nevertheless insisting that there's overwhelming evidence that, however it came to be, it certainly wasn't created by the all-powerful, all-knowing, all-good God of Christian theology. It may be that they can be as justifiably confident of that as they can be that it is not the creation of an all-powerful, all-evil god. Which is something almost all of us are rightly confident about.

An atheist 'leap of faith'?

But don't we *all* have to make a 'leap of faith' at some point – atheists included? Atheists, after all, believe they inhabit a physical world filled with trees, houses, mountains, and people. But they believe this only because that is the kind of world their senses appear to reveal. So how can they know their senses are a reliable guide to the truth? How can they know that their experiences are produced by a real world, rather than, say, a supercomputer generating a sophisticated virtual reality, as in the film *The Matrix*? After all, everything would seem exactly the same, either way. So atheists cannot justify their belief that their senses are fairly reliable. Their belief that the world they seem to experience is real involves a huge leap of faith.

Now it seems to many Theists that they directly experience God. So why shouldn't they place their trust in this God experience, in the same way atheists place their trust in their perceptual experiences? Neither, it seems, can justify their beliefs based on these experiences. Yet we do not normally consider the atheist's trust in the reliability of his or her senses to be unreasonable. But then, why should we consider the Theist's trust in the reliability of his or her religious experiences to be any less reasonable?

Further, the Theist might claim that, precisely because they do place their faith in their God experience, they don't then have to place any *additional* faith in the reliability of their normal perceptual experiences. If there is a benevolent God of the sort the Theist seems to experience, that God will not allow them to be systematically deceived by their senses. So trusting their senses does not require a further leap of faith.

So, the Theist may conclude, at least for someone who has such religious experiences, belief in God need be no more or less a faith position than is the atheist's belief in the external world.

This is an ingenious line of argument. It may contain *some* truth. It might be true that atheism is a faith position because *any* belief one holds about how things stand outside of one's own mind is ultimately a faith position (though I have my doubts even about this – for example, some philosophers argue that the view that physical objects, other people, and so on exist outside my own mind is the *best available explanation* I possess for various perceptual experiences I have, and is thus not a faith position at all, but a well-confirmed hypothesis).

However, even if any belief about how things stand outside one's own mind requires a leap of faith, it does not follow that it is as reasonable for Theists to place their trust in their God experiences as it is for atheists to trust their normal perceptual experiences.

Here's one obvious difficulty with the suggestion that trusting a supposed experience of God involves no greater leap of faith than trusting the deliverances of your other senses.

Observation reveals that people have a very diverse range of religious experiences. Some believe that, through such experiences, they know that there are many gods, some one god, and some (such as some Buddhists) no gods at all. Some experience the Judaeo-Christian God, others Thor, others Zeus, others Mithras, and so on. People have experienced literally thousands of gods and other supernatural beings (saints, angels, ancestors), beings with a huge and diverse range of characteristics. The existence of any one of these gods typically rules out the existence of many, and in some cases all, of the others. So we know that at least *many* of these experiences must be at least *in large part* delusory. But then isn't someone who, knowing all this, nevertheless insists that their own particular religious experience is a reliable indicator of the truth being very credulous – far more credulous than someone who merely takes their normal sensory experiences to be fairly reliable (for at least our normal senses don't provide us with good evidence that they are not themselves fairly reliable)?

A second difficulty with the above suggestion is that while the Theist's assumption that they experience God might then lead them to trust the deliverances of their other senses, their other senses then *quickly furnish them with ample evidence that there is no such benevolent being* (see the problem of evil above). So, unlike the assumption that our normal senses are pretty reliable, the Theistic assumption actually ends up *undermining itself*.

The apophatic theologian

Some Theists will be unmoved by the kinds of argument discussed in this and the previous chapter. They may say something like this:

> The God that you don't believe in, I don't believe in either. You are working with an outdated and unsophisticated conception of God. 'God' is the name I give to whatever is the answer to the question 'Why is there anything at all?' – which is something unknowable, ineffable, beyond our understanding. We can say what God is not – that God is not literally a 'thing' or 'person', for example. But we cannot say what God is.

The view that we cannot say what God is, only what God is not, is sometimes termed *apophaticism*. Apophatic theism has its attractions, perhaps the most obvious being that, if you never say what God is, you can never be contradicted or proved wrong.

At first sight, apophatic theism appears to make atheism impossible. For example, say, 'There is no such thing as God', and the apophatic theist will actually agree with you – 'Yes, there is indeed no such *thing*!'

The theologian Denys Turner is a leading exponent of this sort of theism. In his inaugural lecture as Professor of Divinity at Cambridge University (entitled 'How to be an Atheist'), Turner says to the atheist:

> It is no use supposing that you disagree with me if you say, 'There is no such thing as God'. For I got there well before you. What I say is merely: the world is created out of nothing, that's how to understand God. Deny that, and you are indeed some sort of decent atheist. But note what the issue is between us: it is about the legitimacy of a certain very odd kind of intellectual curiosity, about the right to ask a certain kind of question.

Note Turner's parting suggestion, here, that *the* issue between the atheist and a theist like himself is whether a deep curiosity about such questions as 'Why is there something rather than nothing?' is even legitimate. Turner goes on to characterize the atheist as someone who isn't engaged by such questions, who remains steadfastly unamazed and unperplexed by the fact that there is anything at all.

But if *that's* what an atheist is, then I am not an atheist, and neither are most philosophers (which will come as a surprise to very many of them).

Of course, most apophaticists aren't just expressing wonder and advocating philosophical reflection. Indeed, even while professing ignorance, they often have an awful lot to say about God, even if it is heavily qualified and couched in the language of analogy and metaphor. For example, Turner himself says above that the world was *created* from nothing, rather than that it was caused, or just appeared, from nothing. But as the thought that the world is created tends naturally to lead one on to the thought that it has a creator or cause, it looks as if Turner is here gesturing towards something at least *analogous to* a transcendent agent or cause. In which case, he is gesturing towards something atheists can begin to get their teeth into.

And of course, many apophatic theists also deem this mysterious, transcendent whatever-it-is worthy of our worship and gratitude, which raises the question of how, if it is really unknowable, they can possibly be in a position to *know* that worship and gratitude are appropriate attitudes for us to have towards it?

In fact, if Turner is right and the world is created, doesn't the appalling amount of suffering it contains give us excellent grounds for adding two more characteristics to the list of those apophaticists who say their God *is not* – their God is not worthy of either our worship or gratitude.

Conclusion

In the preceding chapter, we saw that several of the most popular arguments for the existence of God are poor. We also saw that it is by no means obvious that the universe is the creation of some sort of transcendent super-person or super-intelligence even makes sense.

In this chapter, we have seen that there is, in addition, a further powerful challenge to belief in the traditional God of monotheism – the evil god challenge. Because I cannot see how this challenge can be met, I believe there is no such God.

Chapter 4
Humanism and morality

Among the 'big questions' humanism addresses are moral
questions, questions about what we *ought*, or *ought not* to do.
Humanists believe in right and wrong. Indeed, many are
passionate in their ethical commitments.

However, many religious people question the claim that morality
is something those who reject belief in God can even allow for.
Three kinds of challenge tend to be raised. They are as follows:

First, *how can there be good without God?* Surely, in talking about
things being morally 'right' or 'wrong, we are helping ourselves to
an objective, God-given yardstick against which such values might
be measured. If there is no God, then there is no such yardstick,
and so such talk can amount to little more than expressions of
personal preference. Morally speaking, we can all do whatever we
like.

Second, *how can we know what is good without God and religion
to guide us?* Surely, without the moral compass religion provides,
we are left all at sea, no longer able to get our moral bearings.

Third, *will we be good without belief in God?* Surely we behave
ourselves only because we believe there is a God who knows
what we are up to, and who will judge us and punish us if we do

7. Moses bringing God's Commandments down from Mount Sinai. According to some religious people, morality must come from God

wrong and reward us if we do good. It is important people believe God exists, if only to keep them on the straight and narrow.

This chapter begins by taking a closer look at these three challenges.

Can there be good without God?

One of the most popular arguments that, without God, morality is impossible, runs as follows.

Morality cannot come from us. It cannot be our own creation. If it were, that would make morality both arbitrary and relative – which it is not.

Why arbitrary? Because, if prior to our decreeing that anything is right or wrong, there *is* no right or wrong, our decrees cannot be based on moral reasons. Whatever judgement we make must be, morally speaking, an entirely arbitrary one.

Why relative? Well, if what is morally right or wrong is determined by what we say, then, had we said that torturing the innocent is right, it would have been. Indeed, for those of us who say it is right, it *is* right. What is right or wrong is entirely relative to whatever we decree.

But surely morality is not arbitrary and relative in this way? We can't make torturing innocent people right just by saying so. Such torture is wrong *period*, not just wrong-because-we-happen-to-say-so.

But, concludes the argument, if things are not right or wrong because we say so, then they must be right or wrong because God says so. Why is torturing the innocent wrong whatever we might happen to say or think about it? Because God says it is wrong.

The theory that things are morally right or wrong, good or bad, only because God says so is known as *the divine command theory*. According to the divine command theory, the wrongness of murder simply consists in the fact that God commands us not to do it.

The Euthyphro dilemma

The above argument for the divine command theory is seductive and popular. However, it is, on closer examination, a poor argument. A key flaw in it was first exposed by the philosopher Plato in his dialogue *Euthyphro*.

The flaw in the argument becomes clear when we ask:

> Are things morally right/wrong good/bad because God says so, or does God say that they are right/wrong good/bad because he recognises that they are?

Which of these two answers should the theist give? If the theist says things are morally right or wrong only because God says so, then morality, it turns out, is *still* arbitrary and relative. Prior to God's issuing any commands, there is no right or wrong, and thus whatever commands he issues must be morally arbitrary. Moreover, had God said torturing the innocent was right, then it would have been. But of course, this claim is just as counter-intuitive as is the claim that had we said torturing the innocent was right, then it would have been. We face the same difficulties all over again, only now at the level of God.

In response, some theists insist that, as God is himself morally good, he wouldn't command us to torture innocent people. However, according to the divine command theory, to say that God is morally good is just to say that God says he is good, which is something he can say whatever commands he issues regarding torturing the innocent. So, on the divine command theory, God's goodness would not entail that he wouldn't command us to torture the innocent.

It appears, then, that the first answer – things are morally right/wrong because *God* says so – is as unacceptable as the claim

74

that things are morally right/wrong because *we* say so, and for much the same reasons.

What, then, about the second answer: God says things are morally right or wrong because he himself recognizes that they are? God does not make torturing the innocent wrong by virtue of issuing his commands. Such torture would be wrong whatever God commanded. God's commands are issued, as it were, for informational purposes only.

Some divine command theorists, recognizing the seemingly insurmountable problems facing the first answer, plump for the second. But notice that if the theist opts for the second answer, then *the original argument that morality depends on God's commands collapses*. The theist is now acknowledging that torturing the innocent is wrong *anyway* – it's *objectively* wrong – whether or not there exists a God who issues commands. But then atheists and agnostics are free to help themselves to this same objective moral yardstick. They are no more obliged to say that morality boils down to subjective preference than is the theist.

None of this is to deny that there is a puzzle about the objectivity of morality – about how it is possible for things to be morally right or wrong independently of how we, or even God, might judge them to be. My point is that the divine command theory does not provide a genuine solution to this puzzle.

Identifying God with good

This by no means exhausts all the arguments a theist might offer for the conclusion that there cannot be good without God. Here's a rather different suggestion. Suppose moral value is non-arbitrary and non-relative. Suppose there is, as it were, an objective moral standard or yardstick. And now suppose that 'God' refers, not to the *creator* of this yardstick, but to *the yardstick itself* (or, if you prefer, to one end of it – the good end). But *then to admit that there is an absolute standard of right and wrong is just to admit that God exists.*

This is a nice sleight of hand with words. If *all* that the theist means by 'God' is some objective moral standard, then of course, by admitting there is such a moral standard, one thereby admits that God, thus understood, exists. However, this is a very thin understanding of what 'God' means. Many atheists will happily concede that, if that is all the theist means by 'God', then they believe in God! But of course, theists usually operate with a much thicker notion of 'God'. They typically understand 'God' to refer, not *just* to such a moral standard, but also to any number of the following: the creator of the universe; a designer; an intelligence; an agent who knows things, has intentions, and feels emotions such as jealousy, anger, love, and so on; a person in whose image we are made; a worker of miracles; an historically situated human being that died and came back to life; the ultimate author of the Koran; an oracle or revealer of truths; someone offering us the promise of eternal life; and so forth. To claim there is an absolute moral standard is not to commit yourself to any of these other claims, whether they be literally, or merely analogically, understood. But then to accept that there is an absolute moral standard is *not* to accept that 'God' exists, on any thick understanding of that term.

How are we to *know* what is right and wrong?

Let's now turn to the second challenge: how can we *know* what is morally right and wrong without God and religion to guide us? Suppose there is an objective moral standard – how are we to know in which direction it points? Surely, whether or not the divine command theory is true, we still need religion and God to inform us about right and wrong? Where do humanists go for moral guidance?

8. Like it or not, the responsibility for making moral decisions has a boomerang-like quality. Try to pass it on if you like, but it always comes back to you

Humanists can and do acknowledge that some people may be more 'expert' than others when it comes to morality, in the sense that they may possess greater moral knowledge, and may be more reliable judges of right and wrong. Clearly, some individuals and some texts may possess important moral wisdom.

Where the humanist differs from many religious people is in the attitude they take, and encourage others to take, towards such resources. Some insist that one particular group of resources is privileged, and that the core morality it promotes should be accepted more or less without question. Humanists, by contrast, stress the importance of our *individual moral autonomy*.

Of course, humanists don't suppose we should be free to *do* whatever we like. They acknowledge our society requires laws, a police force, and a judiciary. But they suppose we should be free to *think* for ourselves, to make our own moral judgements and (short of inciting mindless violence or suchlike) express our own opinions. They deny that we should each hand over responsibility for making moral judgements to some external authority, such as a political or religious leader.

You might wonder about that. Surely, we often are justified in handing responsibility for making judgements over to an expert? No doubt you go to a doctor for a medical opinion, to a plumber for expertise on central heating, and so on. It is often reasonable just to take the authority's word for it in such cases.

So why not accept the judgement of, say, a religious authority on moral questions? If they have devoted their life to thinking deeply about moral issues, why not defer to their expertise?

That would certainly be convenient. But, unfortunately, morality is not like, say, medicine or chemistry. If a professor of chemistry advises a new student to dispose of a lump of potassium down a sink, and another student is killed in the resulting explosion, the first student is not to blame – the expert is. But if a religious teacher advises their new student to kill anyone who rejects their religion, and the student obeys, the student is culpable. Assuming they have not been coerced or brainwashed, they are responsible for the deaths. Intuitively, they cannot absolve themselves of responsibility by saying, 'But my religious leader told me I should do it' in the same way the chemistry student can absolve themselves of responsibility by saying 'My chemistry professor told me I should do it'. The responsibility for making moral judgements has a boomerang-like quality: try as you might to hand it over to some expert, it seems it always comes back to you.

Of course, the suggestion that we ought to make our own minds up about right and wrong, rather than defer to religious authority, will strike many as outrageous. 'The arrogance!' they may say. 'You are *playing God*. When it comes to answering moral questions, we must rely on religion.'

But, like it or not, playing God cannot be avoided. Even if I decide to follow what is said in some holy book or by some priest, I must still, nonetheless, make my own judgement. For I must still judge which religious book, which parts of the book, which interpreter of the book, and so on I should pay attention to. Such judgements are unavoidable. Even just sticking with the religious teaching with which I was raised requires that I make them. And they are themselves moral judgements. They involve the question, '*Ought I* to follow the moral advice I have been given?'

Each individual has inevitably to rely on their own individual moral compass – their own sense of right and wrong – in weighing up to whom they should listen and whether or not to accept the moral advice they are given. This is as true for theists as it is for humanists.

Will we be good without God?

I now turn to the third of our three challenges: will we be good without belief in God? Many believe that if religious faith is undermined, morality will collapse and the fabric of society will unravel. Humanism is, therefore, a dangerous idea.

That claim is often made, but what evidence is there that it is true? One of the most popular arguments focuses on a *correlation* – between, on the one hand, a decline in religious belief, particularly since the middle of the 20th century, and a supposed increase in various social ills over the same period – including the incidence of crime, delinquency, and sexually transmitted disease. It is suggested that this correlation is no accident. There is more crime, delinquency, and sexually transmitted disease *because* there is less religion. The latter is the main *cause* of the former.

But is it true that our society is far less moral than it was back in the 1950s? Yes, we have rather different moral attitudes. But that is not necessarily a bad thing. In the 1950s, homophobia and racism were rife, and many thought a woman's place was at the kitchen sink. We have actually seen some huge moral improvements over the last half-century or so.

Still, there is evidence to suggest that, at least in *some* respects, we are worse off. For example, in the UK, about six million crimes are recorded each year. In 1950, the figure was half a million. In the United States between 1960 and 1992, citizens experienced a five-fold increase in the rate of reported violent crime (murder, rape, robbery, aggravated assault). Even taking into account differences in the way crime is reported, it is clear there has been a significant increase. Can't this be put down to a loss of religious belief?

Not easily. In fact, while violent crime is up since 1950, it is actually hugely down (50 times less) compared to a couple of centuries ago, when our society was very religious indeed. So higher levels of crime clearly can and do have causes other than reduced levels of religiosity (if, indeed, reduced religiosity is a cause at all).

In fact, there are many obvious changes that have taken place over the last half-century or so that might well explain a rise in crime. For example, people are much more mobile, homes are more likely to stand empty during the day, and people are less aware of who their neighbours are and what they are up to. Tightly knit local communities are effective at suppressing crime and delinquency. Their loss has at least as much to do with changing economic circumstances than a decline in religious belief and practice.

So it is by no means obvious that a loss of religious belief is the cause of a rise in crime. The mere fact that two things happen at the same time does not establish a causal connection (to suppose otherwise is to commit the *post hoc* fallacy).

Indeed, a closer look at the evidence strongly suggest that loss of religious belief is *not* the main cause of the increase in these social ills. When we look across the world's developed democracies, we find that those that are *most* religious – including, of course, the United States (where 43% of citizens claim to attend church weekly) – tend to have the *highest* rates of homicide, sexually transmitted disease, abortion, and other measures of societal health, with the least religious countries, such as Canada, Japan, and Sweden, among the lowest. If declining levels of religiosity were the main cause of such social ills, we should expect those countries that are now least religious to have the greatest problems. The reverse is true.

Not only is there little evidence to support the view that without religion, civilizations risk moral collapse, there is considerable evidence against it. As Francis Fukuyama (the thinker probably best known for declaring the 'End of History') points out, China also provides an important counter-example to the view that moral order depends on religion:

> The dominant cultural force in traditional Chinese society was, of course, Confucianism, which is not a religion at all but rather a rational, secular ethical doctrine. The history of China is replete with instances of moral decline and moral renewal, but none of these is linked particularly to anything a Westerner would call religion. And it is hard to make the case that levels of ordinary morality are lower in Asia than in parts of the world dominated by transcendental religion.

Indeed, from the point of view of other cultures, the widespread Western assumption that people won't be good without God is baffling, as the Chinese writer and inventor Lin Yu Tang here points out:

> To the West, it seems hardly imaginable that the relationship between man and man (morality) could be maintained without reference to a Supreme Being, while to the Chinese it is equally amazing that men should not, or could not, behave toward one

another as decent beings without thinking of their indirect relationship through a third party.

There is also a growing body of scientific evidence that our morality is, to some degree, a product of our natural, evolutionary history. Certain moral attitudes are universal. The world over, people have the same basic moral intuitions about stealing, lying, and killing, irrespective of whether or not they are religious. Pretty much every society is drawn to something like the Golden Rule: do as you would be done by. Why?

There is evidence that our moral intuitions about what we ought, or ought not, to do were, at least in part, written into our genes long before they were written down in any religious book (I recommend Matt Ridley's *The Origins of Virtue*; Robert Wright's *The Moral Animal*; and Richard Joyce's *The Evolution of Morality* for useful overviews and discussions of the evidence). Religion did not create morality. Rather, religions merely codify the kind of basic morality to which humans are naturally disposed anyway. Our initial impulse to behave morally is, it seems, natural and instinctive, rather than acquired through exposure to religion.

Religion – positive social effects

There is little doubt that religion has helped some people turn their lives around. I have heard anecdotes about convicts who have 'found God', and, as a result, have stopped committing crimes and started helping others. No doubt exposure to religion has had dramatic effects on some people's behaviour, particularly individuals who have hitherto led deeply troubled and destructive lives.

However, the extent to which it is religion *per se* that has this redeeming effect, rather than, say, exposure to people who show a genuine interest in the prisoner and their welfare, is debatable (we should also remember that plenty of prisoners have also found the same sort of redemption through philosophy or education; it might even turn out that these alternatives are actually rather more effective in helping prisoners forge a better life).

Moreover, the observation that religion has had a positive effect on the behaviour of some troubled individuals provides little support for the view we are examining here – that without widespread religion, people won't be good and the fabric of society will unravel. After all, Big-Brother-style torture and brainwashing would probably have an effect in controlling criminal behaviour. That fact hardly supports the view that, without widespread torture and brainwashing, people won't be good and the fabric of society will unravel.

What of evidence that the religious are more likely to be charitable than the non-religious, such as that presented in the book *Who Really Cares?* by Arthur C. Brooks, which suggests that the religious are approximately 25% more likely than the non-religious to donate money to charitable causes, including non-religious causes (though note that, as 40% of American Christians will say they attended church last Sunday, when it's been established – by a Christian researcher – that actually only 20% did, this statistic concerning charitable giving, based as it is on what American Christians *say* they did, may be similarly unreliable). Such statistics have led some to conclude that, without religion, a healthy society is impossible. But that doesn't follow. The most this statistic reveals is that, on *one* scale of societal health only, a society might be better off if religious than if not. Indeed, we should not forget that, on other, arguably more important, measures of societal health, the more religious Western democracies fare *worse* than those that are less religious.

Religion has no doubt produced *some* social benefits. A stronger inclination to be charitable may even be among them. However, it is possible such benefits might be had without religion. Perhaps the increased tendency to be charitable is a result of religious practice getting people into the habit of thinking about and helping others, something we can otherwise easily forget about. There may be other ways of getting people into such good habits. In Chapter 6, I point to evidence that exposure to certain kinds of philosophy programmes can *also* help inculcate in young people a more caring and considerate attitude to others.

The 'moral capital' move

In order to deal with the, for them, embarrassing observation that across the West, atheists and agnostics are generally behaving rather well (on most measures, at least as well as their religious counterparts), some religious thinkers appeal to the notion of *moral capital.* They suggest that our religious heritage has produced a reserve of moral capital which today's humanists are currently drawing on. Eventually, this capital will run out and moral chaos will ensue. We need quickly to replenish that religious moral capital if we are to avoid disaster.

The expression 'moral capital' is particularly popular among American conservatives. Irving Kristol (often referred to as the 'godfather' of neoconservatism) makes use of it:

> For well over 150 years now, social critics have been warning us that bourgeois society was living off the accumulated moral capital of traditional religion and traditional moral philosophy.

So does Gerturde Himmelfarb, who claims we are:

> ... living off the religious capital of a previous generation and that that capital is being perilously depleted.

Ronald Reagan's Supreme Court nominee Judge Robert K. Bork concurs:

We all know persons without religious belief who
nevertheless display all the virtues we associate with religious
teaching...such people are living on the moral capital of prior
religious generations...that moral capital will be used up
eventually.

The expression continues to crop up regularly in discussions of
religion and morality – and not just in conservative American
circles. In 2006, Bishop Michael Nazir Ali, interviewed on
the *Today* programme, said:

British society is based on a Christian vision and Christian
values...Unless people know what the springs are that feed our
values, the whole thing will dry up...We may already be living on
past capital.

Richard Harries, Bishop of Oxford, wrote in 2007:

...many people who have strong moral commitments without any
religious foundation were shaped by parents or grandparents for
whom morality and religion were fundamentally bound up...How
far are we living on moral capital?

The appeal to moral capital provides religious predictors of
doom with a convenient explanation for the fact that today's
atheists and agnostics tend to behave at least as well as their
religious counterparts. Non-religious folk are living off religious
moral capital, capital that is running out, but has not entirely
run out *yet*.

There are at least two serious problems with this appeal to moral
capital.

First of all, we might ask: what *evidence* is there to suggest that
the 'moral capital' explanation is actually correct? I can see very
little. While religious people often *assert* that we are living off

religious capital that will eventually run out, with potentially disastrous consequences, they typically provide little, if any, supporting evidence or argument.

Second, the moral capital move in any case fails to deal with much of the evidence against the claim that believing in God is a necessary condition of our being good. For example, it spectacularly fails to explain why countries such as China have survived, and sometimes morally flourished, without grounding morality in religion. It also fails to deal with the growing scientific evidence that the impulse to behave morally is at least to some degree natural and instinctive, and not dependent on exposure to religion.

To sum up: in certain religious circles, the claim that people won't be good without God has become a mantra, endlessly repeated to the point where everyone assumes it must be true. Yet it is not well supported by the evidence. Indeed, much of the evidence appears straightforwardly to falsify it.

What is distinctive about humanist morality?

We have been looking at three common challenges to humanism regarding morality. In each case, the challenge has been dealt with. Let's now consider what a distinctively humanist approach to morality might actually look like.

What is the humanist's position on, say, same-sex marriages, or euthanasia, or abortion, or animal rights? There is no humanist position on these issues, any more than there is a religious position. Humanists disagree on these matters, just as the religious do.

So what distinguishes the humanist's moral point of view, if not such specific moral beliefs? Do all humanists sign up to a particular broad theory of morality, for example?

Again, no. True, humanists are often characterized by their opponents as embracing a fairly crude form of utilitarianism, on which the only thing that matters, morally speaking, is maximizing pleasurable experiences and minimizing pain and suffering.

In its simplest form, utilitarianism faces some well-known objections. For example, utilitarianism seems to entail that it would be right to, say, kill one person to supply donor organs that could save several others – an action almost everyone considers morally wrong. Possibly, these objections can be dealt with, but, even if they cannot, they do not entail that humanism is refuted. For, as I say, humanists are not obliged to be utilitarians, and in fact many reject utilitarianism.

Of course, most humanists agree with the utilitarian view that the consequences of our actions – including the pain or pleasure they cause – are important, morally speaking. A humanist is more likely to give greater moral weight to the consequences of actions than would, say, the kind of religious person who believes that (i) morally the right thing to do is to do what God commands, irrespective of the consequences, and/or that (ii) any bad consequences of following God's commands in this life will ultimately be more than adequately compensated for in the next. As a rule, humanists believe that, if a course of action is going to produce a great deal of suffering, that is a fact of moral significance, a fact that should be taken into account when considering whether this action is morally proper.

But to acknowledge that the consequences of our actions – including the extent to which they maximize pleasure and minimize pain – are morally important is not to say these are the *only* things that are morally important. As I say, humanists are not obliged to be utilitarians.

As we saw in Chapter 1, there is a long intellectual legacy on which humanists can and do draw in formulating their commitments and arguments – including their moral commitments and arguments. Some find inspiration in Aristotle's virtue ethics, others in Kant's duty-based ethics.

Many humanists are drawn to something like the following *pragmatic* justification of their basic moral principles. Moral norms serve certain purposes, such as allowing us to live together in relative harmony, facilitating cooperative activity and eliminating harmful conditions. Assuming we want to pursue these goals, there are certain core norms that must be adhered to – which helps to explain the basic norms common to almost every culture, such as prohibitions on stealing, lying, and breaking promises. Given human vulnerabilities, including our inability to survive on our own, some rudimentary set of moral norms is indispensable.

The humanist writer and broadcaster Margaret Knight (1903–83) offers a humanist justification along such lines:

> Why should I consider others? These ultimate moral questions, like all ultimate questions, can be desperately difficult to answer, as every philosophy student knows. Myself, I think the only possible answer to this question is the humanist one – because we are naturally social beings; we live in communities; and life in any community, from the family outwards, is much happier, and fuller, and richer if the members are friendly and co-operative than if they are hostile and resentful.

If there is no general theory of morality to which humanists must, or do, subscribe, what, then, is distinctive about humanist morality? In fact, what marks out a moral point of view as distinctively humanist is *not so much its content as the way in which it is arrived at*. In particular, four features of a humanist moral outlook stand out:

First, as we have already seen, humanists emphasize our *moral autonomy*. A humanist will aim to hold a moral position, not because they have been instructed to, or because someone else to whom they feel an obligation to defer holds it, but because that is the position they have themselves arrived at after careful consideration. This is likely to be a rather more demanding challenge than, say, automatic adherence to a scriptural commandment or the word of a religious leader. Humanists emphasize the importance of helping new citizens develop the kind of intellectual and emotional maturity they will need to tackle this challenge.

Second, humanists *reject moral justifications based on claims of divinely revealed truth.* The humanist obviously won't appeal to scripturally founded doctrines concerning, for example, an afterlife, immortal souls, divine reward and punishment, sin, and so on in justifying their moral positions. A humanist might still morally oppose abortion, but they won't oppose it because they accept, say, the religious doctrine that God attaches an immortal soul to a cell at the moment of conception.

Third, according to the humanist, *morality is essentially tied up with human flourishing* (though not exclusively so – for example, other species matter too). In figuring out what we ought or ought not to do, then, our judgements should be sensitive to scientific and other evidence concerning what will help, or hinder, human efforts to lead rich, happy, and fulfilled lives.

Fourth, humanists *emphasize the role of reason in making moral judgements.* They believe we have a duty to apply our powers of reason as best we can when addressing moral questions. That is not to say that humanists suppose reason alone is capable of determining the answer to any moral conundrum. No doubt that would be naïve. But reason still has an important role to play in, for example: (i) revealing the unacknowledged consequences of a moral position, (ii) revealing logical inconsistencies in a moral position, (iii) revealing when a moral position is based on faulty

9. While reason *alone* may not be able to answer moral questions, it still provides us with an invaluable tool for helping us find our moral way

reasoning, and (iv) revealing certain scientific and other facts relevant to a moral issue (for example, revealing that women are as intellectually competent as men, thereby undermining the argument that women are not intellectually sophisticated enough to merit the vote). Much of the moral progress that has been made over the last few centuries was made because individuals – both religious and non-religious – had the courage to apply their own intellects and question the accepted moral wisdom of the day. By engaging their own powers of reason, they came to recognize that the contemporary treatment of women, or black people, or homosexuals, was based on faulty reasoning, or was inconsistent with some of their most basic moral beliefs. When it comes to making moral progress, reason is an indispensable tool.

Humanism and 'anything goes' relativism

To finish, I want to return to one of the charges commonly made against humanism – a charge with which we opened this chapter – that of moral relativism. If there is a God, it is often said, then things can only be morally right or wrong because *we say so*. But then humanism involves a commitment to a crude 'anything goes' moral relativism on which the truth about right or wrong is whatever we say it is.

The truth, however, is that this is not what humanists believe, and we are now in a much better position to appreciate why.

Yes, humanist morality is very much focused on we humans (and other sentient species), but that is not to say that right and wrong are whatever individual humans, or even human communities, say they are. Individuals, and even entire communities, can be, and sometimes are, profoundly morally mistaken. Almost all humanists accept this.

Indeed, the humanist's commitment to the importance of applying reason to moral questions clearly involves a rejection of the relativist view that moral truth is whatever we say it is. If that kind of moral relativism were true, then there would be *no point* in bringing our critical faculties to bear in figuring out what's right or wrong, because whatever view we end up with would be no more true than the one we started off with.

Of course, some will insist that while humanists may not officially embrace this sort of moral relativism, their worldview nevertheless commits them to it. But again, this is a mistake.

To repeat a point made earlier in this chapter and also in the Introduction – *humanists, as characterized here, need not even be committed to naturalism* (though some are, of course). So while humanists fail to believe in gods and other supernatural agents, they may still suppose that there are more facts than the natural facts, and that the non-natural facts include objective moral facts.

However, even if a humanist does embrace naturalism, it by no means follows that they thereby commit themselves to the view that the truth about right and wrong is whatever we say it is, and thus that 'anything goes'.

We noted above that, according to the humanist, *morality is essentially tied up with human flourishing*. And, as we have seen, human flourishing requires that we collectively sign up to certain basic moral principles regarding stealing, lying, killing, and so on. But then a self-serving individual who says 'I say it's ok for me to steal, cheat, and kill, so it is – everyone else can go hang' cannot be described as embracing a humanist morality.

Chapter 5
Humanism and secularism

What is secularism?

Humanism involves a commitment to secularism. But what is secularism?

The term 'secular' is used in at least two different ways. Sometimes, it means little more than 'not religious'. Often, when people describe a society as becoming 'more secular', they mean only that it is becoming less religious.

However, the word has at least one other meaning. When humanists say they want a 'secular society', they are usually advocating a particular view about how society should be organized politically, a view about what kind of relationship should hold between religion and the state.

A secular society, thus understood, is not necessarily a society in which there is little or no public manifestation of religious belief. A secular society could be one in which everyone is deeply religious, and in which religious points of view are regularly publicly aired. A secular society is simply one in which *the state itself* takes a neutral view with respect to religion. The state does not align itself with any particular religious, or anti-religious, point of view.

A secular state, in the sense we are discussing now, protects certain *freedoms*. It protects the freedom of individuals to believe, or not to believe, to worship, or not to worship. A secular state defends the right of individuals to express religious commitments. But it also protects their right both to reject any religious commitment and indeed to express views critical of religion.

Characterized in this way, secularism and atheism are clearly very different things. An Islamic or Christian theocracy is obviously not secular, because one particular religion dominates the state. But then an atheist state such as Stalin's Russia or Mao's China cannot be described as secular either.

So a secular society is one in which the state is religiously neutral. That is not to say it is neutral about everything. It is not neutral on the importance of protecting certain freedoms. But it is founded on principles framed and justified independently of any particular pro- or anti-religious commitment: principles to which we ought to be able to sign up whether we are religious or not.

A secular society is one in which religious people can feel just as much at home as can humanists. Indeed, many religious people are political secularists (including members of, for example, organizations such as Ekklesia and British Muslims for Secular Democracy). They value the kind of religious freedoms that a secular society guarantees.

Secularism is sometimes characterized by its opponents as the view that the state should publicly gag religious people, only allowing religious points of view to be aired in private. But that would be a caricature of what I, and indeed most people who advocate secularism, mean by the term. The British Humanist Association (BHA), for example, promotes secularism, but it does not advocate preventing individuals and organizations from publicly expressing religious points of view. Indeed, the kind of secularism advocated by the BHA protects the freedom to express such views. It merely denies that religious voices should be given a *privileged* status.

Although many Westerners take their freedom publicly to advocate or criticize religious points of view for granted, this freedom was in many cases hard won, and, across much of Europe, has existed for only a few hundred years. In the West, the secular society is a comparatively recent phenomenon.

It is also worth remembering that many Western states are not *that* secular. The British state, does, of course, guarantee religious freedom. But it does give one religion – the Church of England – a privileged position. For example, it allocates 26 seats in the House of Lords to bishops – all men, of course – who can then use their power to attempt to block legislation that has popular, democratic support, such as the bill on assisted dying. The head of state – the monarch – is also head of the national church. The British state also uses public money to fund religious schools, and insists that, subject to a few minor exemptions, in every state-funded school in England and Wales each pupil on each school day must take part in an act of collective worship, 'wholly or mainly of a broadly Christian character'.

One advantage of a secular society

Why have a secular society? One obvious justification is *pragmatic*. Secular societies developed in large measure because people recognized that there are dangers in allying states with religions. The histories of many modern states have been marred by violence caused by competing religious groups trying to wrestle control of the state from each other: Catholic versus Protestant, Sunni versus Shia, Sikh versus Hindu, Jew versus Muslim. The secular state was eventually recognized as offering a way of reducing that kind of conflict, through all parties agreeing to live under a religiously neutral state that protected *all* their freedoms equally and gave favour to none.

Threats to the secular state

One way in which the secular character of a society can begin to be eroded is if the religious begin to insist their particular religious views are deserving of special, institutionalized forms of privilege or respect. Here are five recent British examples of such claims:

- The state should be affiliated to one particular religion.

- The state should not permit plays, publications, and so on that satirize, or might in some way deeply offend those holding, certain religious beliefs.

- Airlines and schools should not be permitted to uphold dress codes which prevent flight attendants or school pupils from wearing religious symbols, if the individual's religion, or religious conscience, requires it (thus, while the dress codes of schools and airlines may prohibit jewellery, an exception must be made for, for example, crucifixes).

10. **Christians protest the BBC's transmission of *Jerry Springer: The Musical***

- The state should fund religiously affiliated schools that are permitted to discriminate against both teachers and pupils on the basis of religious belief.

- The anti-discrimination laws that apply to everyone else should not apply to, say, adoption agency workers who are Catholic and who are asked to help gay couples adopt children.

In some cases, these privileges already exist.

Many people believe these claims are legitimate. Even some non-religious people have sympathy with at least some of them. But can such claims be justified?

A challenge for anti-secularists

Suppose we cross out the word 'religious' in each of the above five claims, and replace it with the word 'political'. How plausible do you find the results?

- The state should be explicitly affiliated to one particular political party.
- The state should not permit plays, publications, and so on that satirize, or might in some way deeply offend those holding, certain political beliefs.

- Airlines and schools should not be permitted to uphold dress codes which prevent flight attendants or school pupils from wearing political symbols, if the individual's political party, or political conscience, requires it (thus, while the dress codes of schools and airlines may prohibit jewellery, an exception must be made for party-political badges).

- The state should fund political-party-affiliated schools that are permitted to discriminate against both teachers and pupils on the basis of political belief.

- The anti-discrimination laws that apply to everyone else should not apply to, say, adoption agency workers belonging to a racist political party who are asked to help racially mixed couples adopt children.

Most of us, including most religious people, would reject all five claims, and with good cause. There are obvious reasons why the state should not align itself with one political party, no matter how benign and well-meaning that party might be. And of course, we should be permitted to satirize and mock the political beliefs of others, irrespective of the offence caused – that right is a feature of any healthy democracy.

But then the challenge facing those who make the religious versions of such claims, yet reject the political versions, is to explain why these differing attitudes to the two sets of claims are justified.

This challenge can be sharpened by noting that, very often, religious beliefs are political beliefs. Consider, for example, religious beliefs concerning the moral status of the actively homosexual, women's role in society, stem cell research, abortion, jihad, the state of Israel, and our moral and financial responsibilities towards the less fortunate. Such beliefs are all highly political. Indeed, religious organizations are often politically active, forming powerful political lobbies. So why should the addition of a religious dimension to a set of political beliefs entail that those beliefs are then deserving of officially sanctioned privileges they would not otherwise enjoy?

Responses to the challenge

How might those who believe the state should be affiliated to a religion, fund religious schools, and so on, respond to this challenge? If they are not to appear guilty of unfounded prejudice, they need to identify some difference between religious and other beliefs that justifies privileging the former. Let's look at four differences that might be supposed to provide that justification.

One difference between religious and other political beliefs is that the former typically involve reference to a *supernatural agent or agents* (though both Jainism and Buddhism offer exceptions to this rule). But this surely fails to explain why, say, religious beliefs should not be satirized. Some people believe in other supernatural beings such as ghosts and fairies. Yet we don't suppose the state should intervene to prevent such beliefs from being mocked.

A second difference that some suppose justifies the state in treating religious beliefs differently is that religious beliefs are often very *passionately held*. Indeed, people are prepared to die for their religious beliefs. Might this explain why these beliefs ought, then, to be given a special status? On closer examination, this justification also fails. Non-religious political beliefs may be just as passionately held. People are also prepared to die for them. That is true of many communists, for example. So should the state fund communist schools that discriminate against non-communists? And should the state prevent communist beliefs from being satirized? Surely not.

A third difference that some suppose justifies the state in treating religious beliefs differently is that religious beliefs often form part of a person's *identity* in a way that other beliefs – including even their political beliefs – do not. People self-identify as Christian, Muslim, Jew, or Hindu, for example, and often feel a powerful kinship with other members of their religion that often transcends any differences in race, nationality, and so on (admittedly, this is by no means true of all religions, but it is true of some). Membership of political movements and parties, by contrast, is rarely woven into a person's sense of who they essentially are to anything like the same extent (though under certain totalitarian regimes they may be).

There is no doubt that someone brought up to attend regular devotional events, who makes pilgrimages abroad, whose devotional community transcends national boundaries, whose clothing and/or jewellery reflects their deep commitment, who gives time each day to related reading, whose home is hung with related icons and portraits, and who perhaps even permanently marks their body with signs of their devotion, is someone for whom that commitment has become an integral part of their sense of who they fundamentally are. But does the deep, identity-forming dimension to their commitment justify the state giving that commitment special treatment? Clearly not if they are committed Manchester United supporters, many of whom check all of the above boxes. But then, again, why should religious commitment be treated any differently?

It is true, of course that, because some religious people are so passionately committed to their faith, to the point where it has become a part of their sense of who they are, that criticism or mockery of that faith is likely to be taken at a deeply personal level. As a result, they may become particularly enraged, perhaps even violent.

Those critical of religious belief, ought, then, to be careful about how they frame their criticisms. They ought not to engage in entirely pointless mockery or insult – in baiting the fervently religious just for the sake of it. Given the predictable results, that would clearly be irresponsible.

However, it does not follow that the state itself is justified in outlawing criticism or mockery of religious belief. Criticism – and also irony, parody, sarcasm, and lampooning – still has its place. True, satire sometimes amounts to little more than pointless insult, but it can also take the form of great art, presenting us with the truth in particularly arresting and insightful ways (think of the satires of Jonathan Swift, for example).

In any case, banning the mockery of beliefs on the grounds that those holding them are likely to become violent as a result is likely to encourage people to become violent when their beliefs are mocked. The moral drawn will be, 'Get sufficiently enraged and aggressive, and the state will then prevent people mocking *your* beliefs too, whatever they happen to be!' All Swiftian satires will have to be outlawed, unless they happen to be targeted at the beliefs of those of us with milder tempers.

A fourth and somewhat more sophisticated suggestion as to why religious beliefs ought to be given a special status by the state is that the rights and freedoms we enjoy in modern liberal societies grew out of, and were originally justified by, reference to a religious framework and values, and that, unless there is continuing, explicit support for that framework and those values, those rights and liberties are increasingly likely to come under threat. Here, for example, is British philosopher Roger Trigg expressing this worry in his book *Religion in Public Life*:

> As a matter of historical fact, the standards of Western Society have arisen from a Christian background … the urge to respect different beliefs, and value individual freedom, needs to be nurtured publicly, and if religious views initially produced it, there is a question how long it can survive without their explicit support.

Notice that this is a version of the appeal to dwindling, religiously produced 'moral capital' of the sort we examined in Chapter 4. We are living off a religious inheritance – an inheritance that, if not replenished, will eventually run out – with potentially catastrophic results.

Trigg is not claiming that every liberal society requires a religious underpinning to survive. He is making the more modest claim that those liberal societies that originally had a religious foundation are at risk if that foundation is lost. This, thinks Trigg, is a good reason for keeping the religious foundation in place. Trigg asks:

> Why is freedom to be respected, and human equality cherished? These questions have a ready answer in a religious context, since

God, it will be held, has made us equal, cares for us equally, and has given us free-will so as to make reasoned choices. Once the religious context is subtracted, the mere existence of rights can seem more precarious.

Indeed, Trigg argues that, once this religious foundation is lost, there is a real risk that a society will slide into totalitarianism. It is only if the state recognizes that there is something higher – something that can provide a check on its excesses – that the natural tendency of states to drift towards totalitarianism is kept under control.

> [M]any would want to see more overt recognition by the State of the authority of God, because only this, it seems, may provide a limitation on the powers of human institutions.

> [O]nce a State repudiates any religious foundation for itself, it recognizes no check on its powers beyond those it is prepared to recognize.

So Trigg justifies allying Western states with Christian churches on the grounds that this provides a necessary brake on the tendency of such states to become increasingly totalitarian. The justification is ingenious. But does it hold water? I don't believe so.

First of all, it is by no means obvious that Trigg's claim about religion acting as a brake on totalitarian tendencies is supported by the historical evidence. Just over one of my lifetimes ago, much of Europe was overrun by a totalitarian state. How did the Christian churches respond to the growing menace? In many places, church leaders welcomed the arrival of the Nazis.

True, there was the occasional religious protest against the increasingly brutal treatment of Jews. But this should be seen against the wider context of virulent anti-Semitism that the Christian churches had helped propagate.

For example, in 1936, the Primate of Poland issued a letter opposing violence against Jews. An unreservedly good thing for him to do, you might think. But here's an extract:

> It is a fact that the Jews are fighting against the Catholic Church, persisting in free-thinking, and are the vanguard of godlessness, Bolshevism and subversion. It is a fact that the Jewish influence on morality is pernicious and that their publishing houses disseminate pornography. It is a fact that Jews deceive, levy interest, and are pimps. It is a fact that the religious and ethical influence of the Jewish young people on Polish young people is a negative one.

This letter, written by the most senior Catholic in Poland, was read from the pulpit of every Polish Catholic Church in 1936. Even while opposing *violence* against Jews, the letter nevertheless illustrates the kind of contempt in which Jews were held by many European Christians prior to the Holocaust.

Anti-Semitism was also rampant in the established German Protestant churches. Daniel Goldenhagen, in his book *Hitler's Willing Executioners*, reports that one Protestant church publication

> ...would, in the words of a contemporary observer, 'again and again describe the Jews with great zeal as a foreign body of which the German people must rid itself, as a dangerous adversary against whom one must wage a struggle to the last extreme.'...Dissent was rare...One churchman recalls in his memoirs that anti-Semitism was so widespread in clerical circles that 'explicit objection [to anti-Semitism] could not be ventured.'

The Catholic Konrad Adenaur, post-war Germany's first Chancellor, was to say after the war:

> I believe that if the bishops altogether had publicly taken a stance from the pulpit a lot could have been avoided. That didn't happen and there is no excuse for it.

But perhaps Nazi Germany was an exception? What of other totalitarian states, such as Fascist Italy? How did the Christian churches respond to the rise of totalitarianism there? Catholicism was recognized as the sole religion of state. What of the rise of fascism in Spain? How did the Catholic Church resist Franco's overthrow of the democratically elected government? It didn't.

The Christian churches do not have a good track record of resisting European totalitarianism. They have often been content to do business with, and even build alliances with, totalitarian regimes, at least up until the point where those regimes have started to threaten their own interests. Of course, there is one exception to this tendency of Christian churches to work hand-in-glove with totalitarian states, and that is the atheistic communist regimes of Eastern Europe, which the Catholic Church has always worked vigorously to overthrow.

We should also remember that, just over four of my lifetimes ago, the Catholic Church was itself still arranging for the garrotting by the Spanish state of citizens who failed to believe what the Church told them.

The suggestion that affiliating themselves with Christian churches is the best protection European states have against sliding into totalitarianism is not, then, particularly well supported by the historical evidence. If anything, the warning provided by European history is: *don't* rely on the churches to protect us from totalitarianism.

Recognizing something higher than the state

Of course, it is important we recognize that there are principles higher than the state. Most of us, religious or not, recognize that this is true of *moral* principles. What the state decrees is morally right or wrong is not necessarily so.

Now a church *could* be among those offering moral criticism of the state when it begins to slide in a totalitarian direction. There is no doubt that getting into bed with the state might increase the power and authority of a church to act as a curb on state power. The problem is, once a church has entered into such an arrangement, it is much less likely that any such criticism of the state will actually be offered. Once church and state have entered into an arrangement of mutual support, each then has a vested interest in protecting the power and authority of the other. Surely a church is most likely to offer such criticism when it is genuinely independent of the state, rather than working hand-in-glove with it?

Our religious foundations?

What of Trigg's suggestion that our modern liberal values have a religious foundation without which they are likely to be eroded? While it is true that our modern political rights and freedoms were originally often justified in religious terms, that is because, back then, every moral and political position tended to be justified in religious terms. As the authors of the BHA's pamphlet *The Case for Secularism* point out:

> Christianity has been the dominant culture, so it is unsurprising that it has supplied the vocabulary of both sides in most significant moral and social divisions. Those who worked for the abolition of the slave trade argued their case in terms of Christian values – and so did the slave-traders. Many of those who sought to improve the atrocious working conditions in factories and mines invoked Christian values – and so did the factory owners and mine owners. Some at least of those who campaigned for greater equality of opportunity, for the extension of the franchise, or for the emancipation of women, or an end to racial discrimination, invoked Christian values, and so did those who defended what they saw as a divinely ordained and unchangeable hierarchy of status and inequality.

Even if, as a matter of historical fact, our modern liberal values were originally argued for on religious grounds, moral and political philosophers have developed a whole range of justifications on which we can also draw, including the pragmatic justification outlined earlier in this chapter. There is no necessity that our rights and freedoms be justified on religious grounds.

Of course, critics of secularism may insist that these other non-religious justifications just don't work. However, justifications based on the assumption that the Judaeo-Christian God exists look even less credible to the majority of political theorists and philosophers.

We should also note that in a country such as the UK, where a significant and growing number of citizens – one-third – are not even prepared to express a cultural connection with Christianity, the result of giving our core values a specifically Christian justification is that those values are then more, not less, likely to be ignored or rejected by a significant number of citizens. Surely, if we want *everyone* to sign up to certain core values, such as human rights, wouldn't it be better if a religiously neutral justification of those rights were offered instead?

Conclusion

Some, though by no means all, religious people suppose that, when an airline instructs a member of staff not to wear a crucifix, or when a Catholic member of staff of an adoption agency is compelled to offer gay couples the same service they offer others, this constitutes a form of unfair discrimination against those with strong religious convictions. The religious are being unfairly victimized. We are not showing their beliefs proper 'respect'.

But this is not obviously the case. Not if the airline is simply enforcing a dress code that involves a blanket ban on jewellery. Not if the racist staff of adoption agencies are compelled to offer mixed-race couples the same service they offer others. Why should an airline with a dress code that prohibits staff wearing jewellery be forced to make an exception for religious jewellery? And, if we don't allow non-religiously motivated bigots to discriminate unfairly against others, why should we grant religiously motivated bigots that privilege?

I have anticipated four possible answers to the question, 'Why should the state accord religious beliefs privileges it does not extend to other beliefs, such as (purely) political beliefs?' None of the answers examined has proved adequate. Of course, many other answers might be given. This overview is designed to illustrate the point that, while it may strike many of us as 'just obvious' that religious beliefs deserve such special treatment, several of the more obvious justifications that might be given fail. I have yet to discover any better justification.

Chapter 6
Humanism and moral and religious education

A colleague of mine once told me that, as a pupil of a Catholic school in 1960s Britain, she asked in class *why* the use of contraceptives was morally wrong. She didn't express disagreement with the view – she merely asked what the justification for it was. As a result, she was sent to the headmaster to be disciplined. The culture her school fostered, at least so far as moral and religious education was concerned, was one of deference to authority – of passive, uncritical acceptance of religious dogma. My colleague, no longer Catholic, added that, even today, more than half a century later, she still finds herself feeling guilty if she dares to question a Catholic belief. Her upbringing was highly effective not only in censoring her, but also in getting her into the habit of censoring herself. The disposition was so deeply ingrained that it survives to this day, long past the point when her religious conviction evaporated.

Many religions have, historically, focused on instilling such unquestioning, deferential attitudes among the faithful. In some cases, they still do. However, it is not only the religions that stand guilty of straightjacketing young minds in this way. Atheists have been guilty too. The atheists Stalin, Mao, and Pol Pot were all obsessed with policing not just people's behaviour, but, even more importantly, their thoughts too.

Humanists are typically opposed to those traditional, religious approaches to moral education that present morality as a set of facts handed down by authority that individuals must more or less unquestioningly accept. But they are no less opposed to such 'educational' techniques when employed by atheist regimes.

11. Big Brother policed not just people's actions, but their thoughts too. Today, many religious and non-religious people agree that moral education should not be based on fear, and should not be about straightjacketing thought

Broadly speaking, humanists favour a liberal approach to moral education, an approach that emphasizes individual moral responsibility. In Chapter 4, I presented an argument that our individual responsibility for making moral judgements is unavoidable, an inevitable part of the human condition. It is our responsibility to make our own moral judgements, rather than attempt to hand that responsibility over to some external authority – such as a religion or political leader – that will make them for us.

But if that is true, then shouldn't we ensure that we raise young people in such a way that (i) they recognize they each have this responsibility, and (ii) they have the kind of intellectual, social, emotional, and other skills they will need to make the best judgements they can? These are among the hallmarks of a humanist approach.

Many people appear to think that the alternative to traditional religious education is to abandon children to invent their own morality from scratch, to tell them that every moral point of view is as valid as every other, and to allow them to do whatever they like. But that would be a caricature of the kind of moral and religious education that most humanists advocate.

Note, first of all, that encouraging children to think and question does *not* require that we abandon rules and discipline. What humanists advocate in the classroom is freedom of *thought*, not freedom of *action*. No doubt children need discipline, and they need good habits drilled into them. But even while we enforce rules, we can still allow young people the opportunity to question those rules and express disagreement.

Second, note that encouraging children to think and question does *not* mean that we cannot explain to them what we believe, and why we believe it. In fact, there is no reason why a faith school promoting a particular religion should not encourage its pupils to think and question. Its teachers may say: 'This is what we believe, and these are the reasons why we suppose these beliefs are true. We want you to believe it too, but we don't want you to just take our word for it. We encourage you to question, think, and make up *your own* minds.' Humanists will similarly want to persuade their children of the truth of their humanist views, but they won't want children to accept those views passively and unquestioningly.

Third, note that a humanist approach does *not* involve telling children that every moral point of view is as correct as every other. In fact, as we saw in Chapter 4, humanists reject that kind of moral relativism. If every moral point of view is as correct as every other, then there is no point in thinking about moral issues, for the view you end up with will be no more true than the one you start off with. Thinking is a futile waste of time. Humanists, by contrast, suppose that, far from being pointless, thinking and reasoning can help us figure out what really is, and isn't, true.

Philosophy in the classroom

There is no specific humanist method of morally educating new citizens. Many different techniques might be employed to encourage young people to start thinking about moral issues. Precisely what type and level of educational activity humanists recommend will depend in part on the age and ability of pupils.

In encouraging children to think critically and independently about moral issues, we are encouraging them to think philosophically. There is, as we have seen, a long, secular, philosophical tradition on which humanists can draw when looking for resources to help morally educate new citizens. However, philosophy in the classroom need not take the form of educating children about that tradition – about who said what, when, and why (such a history of ideas would probably only be suitable for, or even of interest to, much older children). An alternative approach which has been tried successfully in classrooms goes under such titles as 'P4C' (philosophy for children) or 'community of enquiry'. The approach involves bringing children together in groups in which they engage in structured debate about some particular philosophical conundrum (often chosen by themselves). This kind of activity has been applied across the entire age range, and has produced some measurable benefits.

For example, in 2001–2, the psychologist Keith Topping, in conjunction with the University of Dundee, studied the effects of introducing one hour per week of such a philosophy programme at three primary schools in Clackmannanshire. Teachers were given two days of training. The study involved a whole range of tests, and also a control group of schools without any philosophy programme. This study found that after one year:

- The incidence of children supporting opinion with evidence doubled, but 'control' classes remained unchanged.
- There was evidence that children's self-esteem and confidence rose markedly.
- The incidence of teachers asking open-ended questions (to better develop enquiry) doubled.
- There was evidence that class ethos and discipline improved noticeably.
- The ratio of teacher/pupil talk halved for teachers and doubled for pupils. Controls remained the same.
- All classes improved significantly (statistically) in verbal, non-verbal, and quantitative reasoning. No control class changed. This means children were more intelligent (average 6.5 IQ points) after one year on the programme.

When the children were tested again at 14, after two years at secondary school without a philosophy programme, their CAT

12. Children practising philosophy in the classroom

scores were exactly the same (that is, the improvements that had previously been gained were retained), while the control group scores actually went down. Three secondary schools were involved and the results replicated themselves over each school.

Of course, this is just one study and its results might be questioned, but there is a growing body of empirical evidence that this kind of philosophical activity does have measurable social, intellectual, and emotional benefits for children. It produces not just intellectually, but also socially, emotionally, and ethically more aware and sophisticated individuals.

For example, after Buranda State School, a small Australian primary, introduced into all its classes a philosophy programme along similar lines, it reported that 'significantly improved outcomes' occurred in the social behaviour of the students:

> The respect for others and the increase in individual self esteem generated...have permeated all aspects of school life. We now

113

have few behaviour problems at our school (and we do have some
difficult students). Students are less impatient with each other,
they are more willing to accept their own mistakes as a normal
part of learning and they discuss problems as they occur. As one
Yr 5 child said, 'Philosophy is a good example of how you should
behave in the playground with your friends'... Bullying behaviour
is rare at Buranda, with there being no reported incidence of
bullying this year to date. A visiting academic commented, 'Your
children don't fight, they negotiate'... Visitors to the school are
constantly making reference to the 'feel' or 'spirit' of the place. We
believe it's the way our children treat each other. The respect for
others generated in the community of inquiry has permeated all
aspects of school life.

The educational benefits of such programmes are now also being
recognized by the British government's own school inspectors. For
example, a 2001 report on Colby Primary School in Norfolk said:

A strength is the teaching of philosophy and thinking skills.
In these lessons, pupils learn to listen, consider, and respond
in a mature way to the ideas of others. This work is taken to a
high level and clearly has a positive impact on children's work
across the curriculum, giving them confidence to speak and
discuss ideas.

Of course, those who suspect their brand of religious faith might
not survive early exposure to independent, critical thought are
likely to find all sorts of excuses for protecting their religious
beliefs from such scrutiny for as long as possible. The evidence,
however, suggests that encouraging children to think
independently about the big questions is actually a very good
thing – providing various social, emotional, and intellectual
benefits. Are we really going to allow some schools to discourage
or suppress such activity on religious grounds, with the result that
their children then miss out on these benefits? I can see no
justification for doing so.

Faith schools

Humanists hold differing attitudes to faith schools. Some (though comparatively few, I would guess) believe that faith schools should no longer be tolerated. They may argue that, if we are not going to allow, say, political schools that select on the basis of political beliefs, begin each day with the collective singing of political anthems, have portraits of political leaders on classroom walls, and promote party-political views (schools that, surely, would constitute a threat to any healthy democracy), then why should we tolerate their religious equivalents?

However, many humanists are prepared to tolerate faith schools, just so long as those schools meet certain minimum standards. They may suppose, for example, that even independent faith schools should encourage children to think

13. **Many religions have, historically, focused on instilling unquestioning, deferential attitudes among the faithful**

and question, should expose children to a range of religious and non-religious views (preferably articulated by those who actually hold them), and should make it very clear to every pupil that which religious beliefs they hold is a matter of their own free choice. Currently, many British schools fail to meet even these minimum standards.

It is one thing to tolerate faith schools, quite another to suppose the state should fund them. Almost all humanists strongly oppose the state funding of religious schools. Their secular commitments lead them to suppose that there is no justification for the state giving religious beliefs such a privileged, state-sponsored status. Many find it particularly galling that British humanist taxpayers' money is used to fund religious schools that then refuse entry to the children of humanists.

A further reason to encourage a philosophical approach

There is a further reason why encouraging a questioning attitude, rather than deference to authority, might be a good idea. Jonathan Glover, Director of the Centre for Medical Law and Ethics at King's College, London, conducted research into the backgrounds of those who joined in the killing in places like Nazi Germany, Rwanda, and Bosnia, and also of those who worked to save lives. As Glover explained in an interview in *The Guardian*:

> If you look at the people who shelter Jews under the Nazis, you find a number of things about them. One is that they tended to have a different kind of upbringing from the average person, they tended to be brought up in a non-authoritarian way, brought up to have sympathy with other people and to discuss things rather than just do what they were told.

Glover adds,

> I think that teaching people to think rationally and critically
> actually can make a difference to people's susceptibility to false
> ideologies.

In *The Altruistic Personality: Rescuers of Jews in Nazi Europe*,
Samuel and Pearl Oliner report the results of their extensive and
detailed study into the backgrounds of both those who went along
with the Final Solution and those who rescued victims. They
found that the most dramatic difference between the parents of
those who rescued and those who did not lay in the extent to
which parents placed greater emphasis on explaining, rather than
on punishment and discipline.

> [P]arents of rescuers depended significantly less on physical
> punishment and significantly more on reasoning.
>
> [I]t is in their reliance on reasoning, explanations, suggestions of
> ways to remedy harm done, persuasion, and advice that the parents
> of rescuers differed from non-rescuers.

According to the Oliners, 'reasoning communicates a message of
respect for and trust in children that allows them to feel a sense
of personal efficacy and warmth toward others'. The non-rescuers,
by contrast, tended to feel 'mere pawns, subject to the power of
external authorities'.

Those who suppose religious conviction is our best defence
against such moral catastrophes should note the Oliners' finding
that, while religious belief was also *a* factor, 'religiosity was only
weakly related to rescue'.

The real danger of traditional, authority-based approaches to moral
education is that they encourage moral sheep – unenlightened

citizens who may think and do the right thing, but only because that is what their authority tells them. If a less benign authority then comes along, such unenlightened citizens will lack the intellectual and emotional defences they will need to resist.

If we want to raise citizens who will withstand the slide into the kind of moral catastrophes that marred the 20th century, it seems that our focus should indeed be on moral education. But not of the traditional, authority-based sort. Our focus should be on raising independent, critical thinkers.

Chapter 7
The meaning of life

According to some, questions about the meaning of life are inextricably bound up with questions about God and religion. Without God, it is suggested, humanity amounts to little more than a dirty smudge on a ball of rock lost in an incomprehensively vast universe that will eventually bare no trace of us having ever existed, and which will itself collapse into nothingness. So why bother getting out of bed in the morning? If there is a God, on the other hand, then we inhabit a universe made *for us*, by a God who *loves us*, and who has given us a *divine purpose*. That fills our lives with meaning.

But is God, or religious belief, really a necessary condition of our leading meaningful lives? How, exactly, is the existence of God supposed to make our lives meaningful? And if meaningful lives are possible whether or not there is a God, what makes for a meaningful existence? This chapter examines these and related questions.

What do we mean by a 'meaningful life'?

One of the difficulties we face in giving an account of how humanism, or any other view for that matter, can allow for the possibility of a meaningful life is in identifying what constitutes a meaningful life in the first place. I imagine there is a broad consensus that certain answers won't do.

14. Religions often claim to make our lives meaningful. But might religion sometimes be an impediment to leading a genuinely meaningful existence?

Humanism

First of all, surely there is more to leading a meaningful life than, say, feeling largely happy and content. Someone continuously injected with happiness-inducing drugs might have a pleasurable time, but that wouldn't guarantee a particularly worthwhile or meaningful existence.

Second, there are presumably more ways of leading a meaningful life than just doing morally good works. While leading an exceptionally virtuous existence is *one* way in which one might, perhaps, have a meaningful life, it is not the only way. Many great artists, scientists, explorers, musicians, writers, and sportsmen and -women have, surely, lived meaningful lives, despite not being noticeably more moral than the rest of us (indeed, some have been rather immoral).

It seems that not only is a lifetime spent performing good deeds not necessary for a meaningful existence, neither is it sufficient. Consider a man living under a totalitarian regime who devotes his entire life to helping sick children but only because he fears the terrible consequences of not obeying his orders. Has he led a meaningful life? Despite his good deeds, it is by no means obvious that he has. What this example illustrates, perhaps, is that, in order for your life to be genuinely meaningful, you must exhibit a kind of *autonomy*. You must be self-directed, rather than just following the instructions of another.

I suspect many of us would add that someone might *think* their life had been a pointless waste of time when it was in fact highly meaningful. Conversely, I suspect most of us would allow that someone might *think* their life highly meaningful when in truth it was not.

For example, has a woman who has successfully devoted her life to leading a white supremacist movement thereby led a particularly meaningful existence? She and her followers might think so. But does that guarantee that she has? It seems to me the answer is 'no'. To lead a meaningful life, you need not be particularly moral. But surely, if your life's central project is downright *immoral*, then it cannot give your life meaning. Because of the immoral nature of this racist woman's project, it cannot make her life meaningful (though her life could still be meaningful for other reasons, of course). That, at least, is how my intuitions run (though I acknowledge others will disagree).

Also notice that a meaningful life might presumably end in the failure of its central project. Consider Scott of the Antarctic, who struggled valiantly to be the first to reach the South Pole. Despite his failure, Scott's life is held up by many as a shining example of a life well lived. The same is true of many other heroic failures, including, for example, those Germans who tried, but failed, to assassinate Hitler in order to bring a quick end to the Second World War.

We have seen that there are, perhaps, certain features a life must possess if it is to be meaningful – a not immoral project or goal pursued in a self-directed way, for example. But is this even sufficient? It seems not, as a lifetime spent pursuing a worthwhile goal by an enthusiastic incompetent is often rather more farcical than it is meaningful.

Is the search for *the* meaning of life a wild goose chase?

The above section is intended to illustrate the point that it is rather difficult to provide a watertight philosophical definition of what makes a life meaningful.

Part of the difficulty we face, here, perhaps, is that we assume that in order to explain what makes for a meaningful life, we must identify some one feature that all and only meaningful lives possess: that feature that *makes* them meaningful. But why must there be one such feature? Perhaps the search for *the* meaning of life – this single, elusive, meaning-giving feature – is a wild goose chase. Perhaps the concept of a meaningful life is what the philosopher Ludwig Wittgenstein calls a *family resemblance concept*. The members of a family may resemble each other, despite there being no one feature they all have in common (that big nose or those small ears). Wittgenstein supposes the same is true of, for example, those things we call 'games'. Activities such as backgammon, solitaire, football, chess, and badminton resemble each other to various degrees. But is there one thing all and only games have in common, in virtue of which they are all games? Wittgenstein thinks not:

> Don't say: 'There must be something common, or they would not be called 'games'— For if you look at them you will not see something that is common to all, but similarities, relationships, and a whole series of them at that. To repeat: don't think, but look!– Look for example at board-games, with their multifarious relationships. Now pass to card-games; here you find many correspondences with the first group, but many common features drop out, and others appear. When we pass next to ball-games, much that is common is

> retained, but much is lost. – Are they all 'amusing'? Compare chess
> with noughts and crosses. Or is there always winning and losing,
> or competition between players? Think of patience. In ball-games
> there is winning and losing; but when a child throws his ball at
> the wall and catches it again, this feature has disappeared…
> [T]he result of this examination is: we see a complicated network
> of similarities overlapping and criss-crossing: sometimes overall
> similarities, sometimes similarities of detail. I can think of no
> better expression to characterize these similarities than 'family
> resemblances'; for the various resemblances between members of
> a family: build, features, colour of eyes, gait, temperament, etc. etc.
> overlap and criss-cross in the same way. – And I shall say: 'games'
> form a family.

If Wittgenstein is correct, the search for the one feature all and
only games possess is a wild goose chase. It does not exist. But of
course, that does not entail that either there is, after all, no such
thing as a game, or that what makes something a game must be
some further mysterious characteristic we have yet to identify.

Perhaps we make the same kind of mistake if we assume that, if
meaningful lives are possible, then there must be some one feature
that all and only the meaningful lives share. Our inability to
identify this feature amongst the warp and weft of the earthly
features of our lives may then lead us mistakenly to conclude that
either our lives lack meaning, or else the elusive meaning-giving
feature must be other-worldly.

When we look at lives that are meaningful, and compare them
with those that are not, we may find not a single feature possessed
by all of the former and none of the latter, but a great many factors
that have an impact on meaningfulness, including some to which
we have already alluded: a project freely chosen, a project that is
not deeply immoral, a project pursued with some dedication and
skill, engagement in activities that help or enrich the lives of
others, and so on. The impression that none of these worldly

features are sufficient – that some further, magical, other-worldly ingredient is required if our lives are *really* to have meaning – may in part be a result of our failing properly to register that the concept of a meaningful life, like that of a game, is a family resemblance concept. Talk about '*the*' meaning of life may be symptomatic of this confusion.

Is God required for a meaningful life?

While we might struggle to provide a watertight philosophical definition of what makes for a meaningful life, most of us tend to agree about which lives are meaningful and which are not. There's a broad consensus that, say, Marie Curie, Socrates, and Scott of the Antarctic led highly significant and meaningful lives, whereas a mindless follower-of-orders, or someone who has devoted their life entirely to torturing small animals, has not.

However, some Theists argue that, if there is no God, then *no* life is meaningful – not even the life of a Curie, Socrates, or Scott. Let's look at three such arguments.

1. A moral argument
One simple line of argument that may tempt some is: a meaningful life is a morally virtuous life; but morality depends on God; thus there cannot be meaningful lives without God.

We have already looked at two reasons why this initial line of argument won't do.

First, the lives of many great artists, musicians, explorers, and scientists have surely been highly meaningful, despite the fact that the individuals in question were not particularly moral. While moral lives can be meaningful, meaningful lives need not, it seems, be especially moral (though, as we have seen, it's arguable that their central projects must not be downright immoral).

In which case, even if there were no such thing as morality, a meaningful life might still be possible.

Second, the above argument in any case just *assumes* that morality depends on God, a claim we have already seen is dubious (see Chapter 4).

2. The ultimate purpose argument

A second argument for the conclusion that meaningful lives require God focuses on *ultimate ends or purposes*. Surely, the argument runs, a life has meaning by virtue of its having some sort of final aim or goal. We must be here for some purpose. But only God can supply such a purpose.

Some religious people, for example, maintain that our ultimate purpose is to love and worship God. They suppose that without God, there can be no such purpose, and without such a purpose, life is meaningless.

But is God required for us to have a purpose? It seems not. Each living organism has a purpose, to reproduce and pass on its genetic material to the next generation. We each exist for a purpose, a purpose supplied by nature, whether or not there is a God.

What this example also brings out, of course, is that merely having a purpose is not, by itself, *sufficient* to render a life meaningful. Discovering that nature has designed me for no other purpose than to pass on my genetic material hardly makes my life seem terribly significant. Indeed, my life is, on this measure, no more significant than that of a worm, which has the exact same purpose.

In reply, it may be said that I am overlooking a crucial difference between purposes: those for which we have evolved and those bestowed on us by some higher, designing intelligence. It is the latter, they may maintain, that render a life meaningful. But is this true? No. It is notoriously easy to construct counterexamples involving super-intelligent aliens. Here's one of my own devising.

Suppose humans have been bred on this planet for a reason – to wash the smelly underwear of a highly advanced alien race. The aliens will shortly return to pick us up and take us to their enormous alien laundry. Would this fact, or its discovery, fill our lives with meaning? Hardly.

Perhaps it will be conceded that merely being designed by some higher intelligence for a purpose is not enough to render our lives meaningful. The purpose must be one that we positively embrace and that makes us feel fulfilled. Washing alien undies fails on both counts.

But now suppose the aliens have designed us so that we discover we profoundly enjoy washing their underwear. In fact, once we start work in their laundry, we finally feel fulfilled in a way that we have never felt before. We rest each evening with an enormous sense of satisfaction that we are now doing what we were always *meant* to do. Would this make our lives meaningful? It's by no means obvious that it would (whatever we might happen to think).

In reply, it may be said that I am focusing on a silly purpose, certainly not the sort of purpose God has in mind for us. God made us for a particular purpose: to *love* him. It is this specific purpose that makes our lives meaningful.

But, again, this seems dubious. Suppose a woman wants to love someone who loves her unconditionally in return. It occurs to her that she could have a child for that purpose, and does so. Does the purpose for which this new person is created automatically bestow meaning upon their life? Not obviously. Some of us probably were conceived for such a purpose. Yet few would point to that fact in order to explain why their lives have meaning. I cannot see why

God's creating me to love him would give my life any more meaning.

In fact, isn't creating human beings solely for some end a rather demeaning and degrading thing to do, as a rule? But then, why is God's doing it any different? It is debatable whether, if there were a God of love, he would even *want* to create human beings for a particular purpose.

So the question of how our lives can have meaning is not, it seems, easily answered by appealing to divine purpose. In particular, the question of *how* our possessing a God-given purpose makes our lives meaningful has not, so far as I can see, been adequately explained. More often than not, we are offered, not a clear account of how God's existence makes our lives meaningful, but merely a promissory note that, in some mysterious and unfathomable way, it just does.

3. A divine judgement argument

Here's a third argument. It seems lives don't have meaning just because *we* judge that they do. Presumably, a life devoted solely to kicking other people in the shins at every available opportunity would not qualify as meaningful, even if we all thought it did.

But, the Theist might now add, if lives aren't meaningful simply because *we* judge them to be so, then they are meaningful only because *God* judges them to be so. So a meaningful life requires God after all.

This is a popular argument. Unfortunately, it runs into difficulties similar to those that face the parallel argument that if things aren't morally right or wrong because we judge them to be so, they must be right or wrong because God judges them to be so (see Chapter 4). The Euthyphro dilemma crops up here too. We can now ask:

> Are lives meaningful because God judges them to be so, or does
> God judge them to be so because he recognizes that they are?

The first answer seems ridiculous. Surely, had God judged that kicking people in the shins at every available opportunity is what makes life meaningful, that wouldn't make it so. But the second answer – God merely *recognizes* what makes for a meaningful life – concedes that there are facts about what makes for a meaningful life that obtain *anyway*, whether or not God exists to make such judgements. But then, these are facts to which humanists are just as entitled to help themselves as are Theists. God is redundant.

Does meaning require immortality?

We have not, as yet, found a good argument for supposing a meaningful life requires the existence of God. Let's now set such arguments to one side, and consider a slightly different claim: that, whether or not meaningful lives require God, they do at least require that we be *immortal*. How, Theists sometimes ask, can a life have any meaning or point if it ends in death? True, we may have achievements that outlive us, such as books written, buildings designed, and children well raised. But those books will eventually be forgotten and those buildings will crumble. Our children will soon wither and die. Indeed, the human race as a whole will eventually disappear entirely without trace. But then, without immortality, isn't our existence all for nothing – a pointless waste of time?

It seems to me that, while a longer life might be desirable, it is not necessarily more meaningful. True, if you live longer, you may achieve more, do more good works, and so on. But is a long life exhibiting such virtues thereby more *meaningful* than a shorter version? Presumably not. Nor is it obvious why extending such a life to infinity imbues it with any more meaning.

In fact, it is sometimes in the manner of our death that our lives acquire particular meaning and significance. Someone who deliberately sacrifices their own life to save others is often held up as an example of a person whose life is particularly meaningful. I might add that, if we compare the sacrifice of a religious person who lays down their life thinking they will be resurrected in heaven, and an atheist who lays down their life thinking death is the end of them, surely it is the latter individual who intends to make the greater sacrifice, and whose action is, for that reason, more noble and meaningful.

Even when a life is not sacrificed for others, the manner of its end can often be what marks it out as particularly significant. We rightly admire those who face death with courage and dignity. Death is often an important episode of the story of our lives, an event that completes the narrative of a life in a satisfying and meaningful way. The fact that we die, and that death really is the end, does not make our lives meaningless. Indeed, the finality of death gives us an opportunity to make our lives rather *more* meaningful than they would otherwise be.

Religion versus shallow, selfish individualism

Let's now turn to religious practice. Setting aside the issue of whether God exists, perhaps it might still be argued that religious reflection or observance is required if our lives are not to be shallow and meaningless. Here is one such argument.

It is sometimes claimed, with some justification, that religion encourages people to take a step back and reflect on the bigger questions. Even many non-religious people suppose that a life lived out in the absence of any such reflection is likely to be rather shallow. Contemporary Western society is obsessed with things that are, in truth, comparatively worthless: money, celebrity, material possessions. Our day-to-day lives are often lived out within a narrow envelope of essentially selfish concerns, with little or no time given to contemplating bigger questions. It was religious tradition and practice that provided the framework within which such questions were once addressed. With the loss of religion, we have inevitably slid into selfish, shallow individualism. If we want people to enjoy a more meaningful existence, we need to reinvigorate religious tradition and practice (some would add that we need, in particular, to ensure young people are properly immersed in such practices in school).

There is *some* truth in the above argument. Religion *can* encourage people to take a step back and contemplate the bigger issues. It can help break the hypnotic spell that a shallow, selfish individualistic culture can cast over young minds.

However, religion can itself also promote forms of selfishness – such as a self-interested obsession with achieving one's own salvation or personal enlightenment. And of course, religion has itself been used to glorify material wealth, by suggesting that great wealth is actually a sign of God's favour.

Is it true that *only* religion encourages us to think about the big questions? No. In Chapter 1, we saw that there is another long tradition of thought running all the way back to the Ancient world that also addresses the big questions – a secular, *philosophical* tradition. If we want people, and especially children, to think about such questions, we are not obliged to take the religious route. We can encourage them to think philosophically.

Indeed, as I point out in Chapter 6, there is evidence that introducing philosophy programmes into the curriculum can have a dramatic impact on both the behaviour of pupils and the ethos and academic standing of their schools.

Most contemporary humanists are just as concerned about shallow, selfish individualism as are religious people. They too believe it is important we should sometimes take a step back and consider the big questions. They just deny that the only way to encourage a more responsible and reflective attitude to life is to encourage children to be more religious.

If we really want to encourage young people to *think* about the big questions, philosophy is, arguably, a much more promising approach. The Church of England poses the question 'Is this it?' on billboards and buses, promising those who sign up to their Alpha Course 'An opportunity to explore the meaning of life.' However, when the religious raise such questions, they are often posed for rhetorical effect only. They are asked, not in the spirit of open, rational enquiry, but merely as the opening gambit in an attempt to sign up new recruits. Unlike religion, philosophy does not approach such questions having already committed itself to certain answers (though it does not *rule out* religious answers, of course). Philosophy really does encourage you to think, question, and make your own judgements – an approach to answering the big questions that, in reality, many religions have traditionally been keen to suppress.

The claim that *only* religion encourages us to think about the big questions is not just false, it is rather ironic when made by religions with long and sometimes violent histories of curtailing independent thought.

Do humanists miss out on something?

It may be that we do miss out on *something* if we give up religion. Consider belief in Santa Claus. For the child who comes to believe in Santa, the universe appears wonderfully transformed. From within the perspective of their bubble of belief, the world, come December, takes on new meaning and significance – a rosy, magical glow. There is something it is like, for the subject, to inhabit this bubble of belief – to be a true believer in Santa – something it's very hard to understand if you have never experienced it yourself.

15. For the child who comes to believe in Santa, the universe appears wonderfully transformed. There is something it's like, for the subject, to inhabit this bubble of belief, something hard to understand if you have never experienced it yourself

When the child grows up a bit and the Santa bubble pops, it can be distressing for the child: the rosy glow vanishes, leaving the world seeming rather sad and drab by comparison.

There's no doubt that popping the bubble of religious belief can be distressing for its occupant. The magic and meaning may appear to drain out of the world, leaving it seeming cold and barren. Isn't it better to live inside such a religious bubble if we can?

I don't believe so. If there is no God, then the magical glow the world seemed to take on when viewed from inside the bubble was always an illusion. When the bubble pops, the world might seem a little drabber for a while. But, personally, I would rather see the world as it is, than as I might like it to be.

In fact, isn't an appreciation of what is really important in life actually likely to be obscured by such a bubble? Compare belief in Santa, his workshop at the North Pole, the flying reindeer, and so on. When that bubble pops, those colourful characters all vanish, but what was always most important come 25 December – love, getting together with our friends and family, and so on – are all still in place. In fact, for us grown-ups, wouldn't belief in Santa – and the accompanying activities of posting letters to the North Pole, putting out the mince pie and milk – threaten to be a disabling distraction, preventing us from recognizing what truly matters?

I believe the same is true of belief in gods, angels, demons, an afterlife, and so on. It is true that, without religious belief, we may miss out on *something* – such as on seeing the world as a divinely ruled kingdom, on the comforting promise of being reunited with loved ones after our death. But we may gain rather more – including a more mature and clear-sighted view of what is really valuable and significant in life.

As the writer Douglas Adams once said: 'Isn't it enough to see the garden is beautiful without having to believe there are fairies at the bottom of it?'

Humanism and the meaning of life

Some readers may be feeling short-changed. They may ask: 'But what is the specifically humanist answer to the question: what makes for the meaning of life?' The fact is that there is no official 'humanist answer'.

The truth is that (with a few obvious exceptions, such as lives of religious piety) most humanists tend to agree with the religious about which lives are meaningful and which are not. Like most religious people, they agree that raising good children, pursuing intellectual enquiry with dedication, producing strikingly original and moving art, and so on are all ways in which we can enjoy a meaningful existence. Setting aside reference to the divine, humanists also apply much the same *criteria* in judging which lives are meaningful and which are not.

Humanists merely differ from *some* religious people in supposing (i) that those lives that we generally agree are meaningful are still meaningful even if there is no God or gods, and (ii) that belief in God or gods can actually be an impediment to our living full and meaningful lives, by, for example: leading us *not* to think about the big questions; forcing us to live a certain way out of fear of divine punishment; or wasting our lives promoting false beliefs because of a mistaken expectation of a life to come.

From the humanist perspective, it's what's before us – the rich warp and weft of our worldly, human lives – that really matters.

Chapter 8
Humanist ceremonies

An important service many humanist organizations provide to wider communities is the provision of humanist ceremonies and rituals, most notably humanist funerals, but also humanist naming ceremonies, weddings, and coming of age ceremonies. The British Humanist Association (BHA) publishes guides for people considering humanist ceremonies and provides trained humanist celebrants. Humanist funerals are particularly popular – in 2009, celebrants accredited by the BHA carried out over 7,000 such events. And over 70% of marriages conducted in England and Wales today are non-religious.

What accounts for the growing popularity of humanist ceremonies?

The importance of ritual and ceremony

The mythologist Sir James Frazer, author of *The Golden Bough*, believed that primitive peoples engage in ritualistic activity because they embrace a naïve theory about how the universe works. Take, for example, a tribesman who pushes a knife into an effigy of his enemy. Why does he do this? According to Frazer, because the tribesman supposes this may actually have an effect on his enemy. He believes that by stabbing the doll in this ritualistic way, he may actually cause his enemy to die. People engage in such activity because they believe in what Frazer calls the 'law of similarity': the principle that *like produces like*. According to Frazer, it is because many primitive cultures believe in this law that they sprinkle water on the ground to cause rain, or enact successful hunts before going out on a real hunt. Of course, we moderns have a more scientific and sophisticated understanding of how the world works. We know that water-sprinkling won't cause rain, and that doll-stabbing won't cause an enemy to die.

The philosopher Ludwig Wittgenstein rejects Frazer's explanation of why supposedly 'primitive' people engage in such activity. Wittgenstein argues that the tribesman does not stab the doll because he believes in the law of similarity. After all, says Wittgenstein:

> The same savage who, apparently in order to kill an enemy, sticks a knife into him, really does build his hut of wood and cuts his arrow with skill and not in effigy.

Surely, if the tribesman really believed in the law of similarity, then he would believe that by making a little model hut, he could cause a real hut magically to appear. But of course, he has no such expectation. The tribesman does not stab the doll because he believes it will have any real effect. He does it for some other reason. But what?

According to Wittgenstein, this kind of ritualistic behaviour is not primitive, but part of our human nature. It is, to some extent, something we all engage in. We kiss images of ones we love, for example, or angrily tear up photos of those we hate. We touch wood for luck. Even atheist footballers look to the heavens and raise their arms imploringly when they miss a penalty. Why?

> Burning in effigy. Kissing the picture of a loved one. This is obviously not based on a belief that it will have a definite effect on

the object which the picture represents. It aims at some satisfaction and it achieves it. Or rather, it does not aim at anything; we act in this way and then feel satisfied.

The reason we, say, throw darts at photos of those we hate is not that we believe in the law of similarity and suppose that by doing so we will have a corresponding effect on the people concerned (if such rituals worked, Margaret Thatcher, a favourite dartboard pin-up of the 1980s, would now be peppered with tiny holes). Rather, such activity allows us to express deeply felt emotions. It can console us, inspire us, and help make us more resolute.

I believe Wittgenstein is at least partially correct. People who engage in ritualistic activity certainly *need not* suppose that such activity will, or even might, have some sort of magical or supernatural result (though, unlike Wittgenstein, I think some of them do – surely *some* people who pray really do believe there is someone up there listening, someone who might supernaturally intervene on their behalf?). Such activity is not essentially religious. People engage in it all the time, both inside and outside of religious contexts.

Of course, religion has traditionally provided the main framework within which organized ritual has taken place. The formal nature of these rites and ceremonies has traditionally played an important role in, for example, reuniting displaced family members, fostering a sense of kinship and belonging, allowing people collectively to articulate their deepest commitments and desires.

As religion has gone into decline across much of the West, so there has been a loss of opportunity to engage in such organized activity. But of course, the needs for which such activity caters are still there. Such needs are felt particularly strongly when it comes to the great milestones of life – such as birth, marriage, and death. It is not surprising, then, that non-religious people look for alternative rites and ceremonies at such times.

In providing such rituals, are humanist organizations setting themselves up as alternative religions? No. To engage in such activity is not to commit oneself to the existence of gods, or magical beings or powers, or any sort of supernatural reality. Humanist organizations are merely catering for deeply felt emotional needs, needs that form an inextricable part of our human nature.

Humanist weddings

Currently, unlike in countries such as Norway or Scotland, in England and Wales humanist weddings have no legal status, and so, in order to be legally married, couples must also arrange a civil wedding conducted at a register office. However, most couples who marry in this way consider the humanist ceremony to be their 'real' wedding, the wedding at the registry being a mere legal formality.

There is one obvious advantage to having the humanist wedding independently of the legal wedding – in England and Wales, legal

16. A humanist wedding ceremony

weddings can only take place at registered locations, such as register offices, churches, mosques, and synagogues. Humanist weddings, on the other hand, can be conducted anywhere that is practicable. My wife and I were married by a humanist celebrant in the open air on the mound of a ruined castle in Northumberland, surrounded by a large group of friends and family. Of course, I am biased, but I thought it a wonderfully happy and moving occasion, at least as graceful and meaningful as any religious marriage service I have attended.

Humanist funerals

Humanist funerals are conducted without any suggestion that the deceased has merely 'passed on'. They mark the end of a life, not some supposed transition to another mode of existence. Humanist funerals offer friends and family an opportunity to celebrate a life with honesty, dignity, and both sadness and joy, but without any questionable promises of meeting up again beyond the grave.

One reason why humanist funerals, in particular, have become more popular may be that, while many non-believers, in order to have the traditional spectacle of 'walking up the aisle', are prepared to put up with the ceremonial expression of beliefs they don't in fact hold, there is an understandable desire not to have a funeral ceremony out of keeping with the beliefs of the deceased and those they leave behind. As Tana Wollen, BHA Head of Ceremonies, comments:

> Committing the dead to a god or gods that you don't believe exists or sending them off to an after-life you believe is fictional, even with the accompaniment of a sonorous liturgy, doesn't feel right.

Another reason for the growing popularity of humanist funerals may be that the religious versions have traditionally focused primarily on glorifying God, with the deceased sometimes getting scarcely getting a mention. Humanist funerals, by contrast, are primarily a celebration of the life of the person who has died, and, in comparison to traditional religious rites, offer far more opportunity for friends and relatives to express their own emotions and pay tribute to the human whose life has now ended.

It was suggested to me recently, I think with some plausibility, that the increasing popularity of humanist funerals has had a knock-on effect on how religious funerals are now conducted. In Britain today, even religious funerals tend to focus rather more on celebrating the life of the deceased than used to be the case. They too often give friends and relations much more opportunity to pay tribute to and celebrate the life of the deceased person, and perhaps even to choose non-religious music and readings if they are felt to be more appropriate. Indeed, some religious funerals are now barely distinguishable from their humanist counterparts, other than they happen to be conducted by someone wearing religious garb.

Not everyone approves of this trend. A Kent priest, Father Ed Tomlinson, recently expressed his dismay at the number of funerals he leads with little or no Christian content. In his view, the purpose of a Christian funeral service is twofold:

> Firstly to offer an opportunity to say goodbye and secondly to offer loved ones into the hands of a living God, praying that sins may be forgiven and that they may be granted eternal life…What I often bemoan is that this latter point is slipping away, being wholly eclipsed by the former.

Father Tomlinson also questioned the quality of humanist funerals, suggesting the best they can offer is

> a poem from nan combined with a saccharine message from a pop star before being popped in the oven with no hope of resurrection.

Of course, there is no doubt that a humanist funeral service *could* be a shallow and unsatisfying affair. But then, the same is true of religious services. Indeed, to non-believers, religious ceremonies can seem particularly pointless and unsatisfactory if their primary focus is on glorifying God, with little, if anything, said about the shape and quality of the life of the person who has gone. Humanist funerals are often joyous, uplifting, and, I am prepared to say, even spiritual occasions, despite the absence of dubious promises about pie in the sky when we die. In my view, they offer a rather more grown-up version of spirituality.

What humanist ceremonies reveal about humanism

The way in which humanist ceremonies have developed and are conducted reveals a great deal about what humanists consider most important. Humanist funerals, with their personalized, human-centred focus – are a celebration of this life, rather than some mythic life to come. The focus of a humanist wedding is on the expression of the couple's love and commitment, rather than on them entering into some sort of state-enforced or divinely enforced contract. Humanist baby-naming ceremonies focus not on committing the child to a specific god or religion for the rest of their natural life and beyond, but on allowing parents and other close friends and relations to express their commitment to help this new human being flourish – which, for humanists, includes helping them develop the skills and maturity they will need to take on the responsibility of developing their *own* beliefs and making their *own* moral judgements.

One reason why humanist ceremonies are becoming so popular is that people are increasingly recognizing that the humanist vision of what is genuinely most important in life is their vision too.

References

Introduction

The survey indicating the views of professional philosophers on naturalism and theism was conducted by philosophers David Chalmers and David Bourget in November 2009. The results are available at: http://philpapers.org/surveys/, accessed 24 August 2010.

Chapter 1

The Allen Bloom quote is from *The Closing of the American Mind* (New York: Touchstone, 1988), p. 25.

Ruchard Lamm is quoted disapprovingly at http://www.slate.com/id/2100437/ and approvingly at: http://www.christianitytoday.com/ct/2004/119/42.0.html, accessed 24 August 2010.

The Cardinal Ratzinger quote is from his 2005 Homily at the Mass for the election of the Roman Pontiff.

The Nick Tate quote is from a speech to the SCAA on 15 January 1996.

The Cardinal Ratzinger quote on Galileo: Joseph Ratzinger, *Corriere della Sera*, 30 March 1990; *30 Dias*, January 1993, p. 34.

The Alisdair MacIntyre quotes are from Alisdair MacIntyre, *After Virtue*, 2nd edn. (London: Duckworth, 1985), p. 222; and MacIntyre's 'A Partial Response to My Critics' is in J. Horton and S. Mendus (eds.), *After MacIntyre* (Notre Dame, IN: University of Notre Dame Press, 1994), p. 289.

Chapter 2

The Darwin quote is from Charles Darwin, *The Autobiography of Charles Darwin 1809–1882. With the original omissions restored. Edited and with appendix and notes by his grand-daughter Nora Barlow* (London: Collins, 1958), p. 87.

The Behe quotes are both from his *Darwin's Black Box: The Biochemical Challenge to Evolution* (New York: The Free Press, 1996), p. 39.

The Miller quotes are from *The Flaw in the Mousetrap: Intelligent Design Fails the Biochemistry Test.* Published online at: http://www.actionbioscience.org/evolution/nhmag.html, where it is reprinted with permission from *Natural History Magazine* in April 2002, accessed 24 August 2010.

Krauss is quoted from *Free Inquiry*, volume 26, number 3, April/May 2006; and from *Top of Form*, pp. 36–40, available online at <http://genesis1.asu.edu/~krauss/freeinqart.html>, accessed 24 August 2010.

The Hawking quote is from his *A Brief History of Time* (New York: Bantam Books, 1988), p. 125.

The Davies quote is from his *The Goldilocks Enigma* (London: Penguin, 2007), p. 300.

Chapter 3

That around 45% of American citizens (actually, around 135 million citizens) believe the entire universe is around 6,000 years old (polls usually use the phrase 'less than 10,000 years') is supported by a range of polls, such as a 2008 Gallup poll in which 44% of respondents said 'God created human beings pretty much in their present form at one time within the last 10,000 years or so' – for a range of poll results, see http://www.pollingreport.com/science.htm, accessed 24 August 2010.

John Hick uses the expression 'vale of soul making' in John Hick (ed.), *Classical and Contemporary Readings in the Philosophy of Religion*, 2nd edn. (Englewood Cliffs, NJ: Prentice-Hall, 1970), p. 515.

Chapter 4

The Fukuyama quote is from *The End of History and the Last Man* (London: Hamish Hamilton, 1992), p. 328.

The Lin Yu Tang quote is from his *My Country, My People* (London: Heinemann, 1938).

The Kristol quote is from *Neoconservatism – the Autobiography of an Idea* (Chicago: Elephant, 1999), p. 101.

The Himmelfarb quote is from her *One Nation, Two Cultures* (New York: Knopf, 1999), p. 146.

The Bork quote is from his *Slouching towards Gomorrah* (New York: HarperCollins, 1996), p. 275.

The Bishop Ali quote appeared on the *Today* programme on Radio 4, 6 November 2006, and is quoted in BHA's 2007 pamphlet *The Case for Secularism*.

The Bishop Harries quote is from his comment piece 'It is Possible to be Moral without God', published in *The Observer*, 30 December 2007; available online at <http://www.guardian.co.uk/commentisfree/2007/dec/30/religion.world>, accessed 24 August 2010.

The Knight quote is from a talk she gave on the BBC's Home Service (now Radio 4) in 1955 and is available on a webpage at <http://www.humanism.org.uk/humanism/humanist-tradition/20century/margaret-knight>, accessed 24 August 2010.

Chapter 5

The various Trigg quotes are all taken from his book *Religion in Public Life: Must Faith Be Privatized?* (Oxford: Oxford University Press, 2007), pp. 3–4, 73, 12, 125.

David Ranan's *Double Cross: The Code of the Catholic Church* (London: Theo Press, 2006) is the source of the quotations from the Primate of Poland (p. 196) and Konrad Adenaur (p. 218).

Chapter 6

For the Topping study, see S. Trickey and K. J. Topping, '"Philosophy for Children": A Systematic Review', *Research Papers in Education*, Vol. 19, No. 3, September 2004. Also see, e.g., Ofsted reports for schools participating in philosophy for children projects summarized in the document *Extracts from Ofsted Inspection Reports Highlighting the Use of Philosophy*, available from SAPERE.

The Buranda school source is the Buranda State School Showcase 2003 Submission Form.

Jonathan Glover, 'Into the Garden of Good and Evil', *The Guardian*, 13 October 1999.

Much of this chapter draws on my book *The War for Children's Minds* (London: Routledge, 2004).

Chapter 7

The Wittgenstein quote is from *Philosophical Investigations* 1, sections 66–7.

Chapter 8

The Tomlinson quotes come from (i) his blog: http://sbarnabas.com/blog/2009/10/19/clarification-on-funerals/; and (ii) the *Telegraph* website <http://www.telegraph.co.uk/news/newstopics/religion/6375631/Vicar-feels-like-lemon-as-Tina-Turner-played-at-funerals.html>, both accessed 24 August 2010.

The Wittgenstein quotes are from *Remarks on Frazer's Golden Bough* (Oxford: Basil Blackwell, 1975), p. 4.

Further reading

Excellent longer introductions to humanism have been written. Among the best are:

Jim Herrick, *Humanism: An Introduction* (Amherst, NY: Prometheus Books, 2005).

Richard Norman, *On Humanism* (London: Routledge, 2004).

Peter Cave, *Humanism: A Beginner's Guide* (Oxford: Oneworld, 2009).

Paul Kurtz, *What Is Secular Humanism?* (Amherst, NY: Prometheus Books, 2006).

I also recommend the BHA's pamphlet *What Is Humanism?*, available directly from the BHA.

Further information on humanism

The national UK charity promoting humanism is the British Humanist Association (BHA). The BHA campaigns for an open society and a secular state, and provides non-religious celebrations and ceremonies for important events such as funerals and weddings. It has been supporting non-religious people and promoting humanism since 1896, and it works in a wide range of contexts from schools to Parliament to achieve its aims. It provides many resources and educational materials online:

<http://www.humanism.org.uk>

<http://www.humanismforschools.org.uk>

www.humanistlife.org.uk

The Center for Inquiry (CFI) is one of the United States' largest humanist organizations, with branches around the world. It aims to foster a secular society based on science, reason, freedom of inquiry, and humanist values. The CFI website provides many links and resources:

<http://www.centerforinquiry.net/>

The American Humanist Association (AHA) works to establish, protect, and promote the position of humanists, and has a website here:

<http://www.americanhumanist.org/>

The umbrella organization for all humanist organizations internationally is the International Humanist and Ethical Union, which represents 100 humanist, rationalist, secular, ethical culture, atheist, and free-thought organizations in more than 40 countries:

<http://www.iheu.org/>

Index

Expand your collection of
VERY SHORT INTRODUCTIONS